Transformed Christians

too many Christians have the truth on ice instead of on fire.

TRANSFORMED CHRISTIANS

New Testament Messages on Holy Living

by
Milton S. Agnew

Beacon Hill Press of Kansas City
Kansas City, Missouri

Copyright, 1974
Beacon Hill Press of Kansas City

All scripture quotations, except as otherwise indicated, are from the *New American Standard Bible* (NASB), copyright © The Lockman Foundation, 1960, 1962, 1963, 1968, 1971.

Quotations from *The New English Bible* (NEB), © the Delegates of the Oxford University Press and the Syndics of the Cambridge University Press, 1961, 1970. Reprinted by permission.

Quotations from *The Living Bible* (TLB), copyright © 1971, Tyndale House Publishers, Wheaton, Ill. Used by permission.

Quotations from *The New Testament in Modern English* (Phillips), copyright © by J. B. Phillips, 1958. Used by permission of The Macmillan Co.

Quotations from the *Revised Standard Version of the Bible* (RSV), copyrighted 1946 and 1952.

Quotations from *The Amplified New Testament,* copyright 1962-64 by Zondervan Publishing House. Used by permission.

Contents

Foreword	6
Preface	7
Introduction	8
Part I: What Jesus Said	13
1. Christian Perfection (Matt. 5:21-48)	15
2. The Discipline of the Cross (Matt. 16:24-28)	26
3. Perfect Love (Mark 12:28-34)	33
4. The Paraclete (John 14—16)	42
5. Sanctify Them (John 17)	53
Part II: What Paul Said	69
6. Wholly Sanctified (1 Thessalonians)	71
7. God's Pattern for Perfection (2 Cor. 7:1)	82
8. Sin in the Believer (Romans 6—8)	92
9. On Being Crucified with Christ (Romans 6)	99
10. More than Conquerors (Romans 7—8)	106
11. Transformed Christians (Romans 12—15)	111
12. Chosen to Be Holy (Ephesians 1—3)	119
13. The Holy Walk (Eph. 4:1—5:17)	125
14. Spirit-filled Christians (Eph. 5:18—6:20)	132
15. A Sanctified Church (Eph. 5:25-27)	138
16. Resurrection Responsibilities (Col. 3:1—4:6)	143
17. Rekindling the Charisma (2 Tim. 1:6-7)	149
Part III: What Others Said	157
18. The Discipline of Holiness (Hebrews 12—13)	159
19. Be Ye Holy (1 Peter 1—3)	168
20. Victorious Living (1 John 1—2)	179
In Summary	186
Appendix	192
Reference Notes	203
Bibliography	206

Foreword

This very fine book, written by Colonel Milton S. Agnew, is both challenging and highly informative, and I am sure it will help many Christians toward the achievement of that maturity Christ calls for by the indwelling Spirit.

I tried to imagine the author's experience through the five years' devoted labor in translation of the New Testament. I wish I had the knowledge and skill to engage in a similar enterprise; for though many have undertaken such a translation, to be able to do it for oneself would be singularly rewarding, as he writes in his preface. The insights gained through this labor of love have been amply revealed in *Transformed Christians.*

Today, probably more than any time in the past, we must emphasize holiness teaching in order to help anchor God's people securely in the Faith; for eroding forces within our society, including the philosophy that permeates much of the education process, are nibbling away at Christian essentials.

We are indebted to Colonel Agnew for this eloquent and competent work. This book is worthy of wide circulation, and I am sure it will bring much spiritual blessing to those who read it.

London, England —CLARENCE D. WISEMAN
July 30, 1974   *General, The Salvation Army*

Preface

In a five-year, painstaking translation of the entire New Testament from the original Greek the writer rediscovered a whole series of essays or "expository thoughts" by Jesus and then by His apostles on the subject of holy living and holiness.

A common theme of truth appeared from the whole, sometimes emphasizing one aspect and sometimes another, but remarkably compatible, uniform, and sensible, threading the whole of the New Testament, and reflecting the doctrine of the atonement in its fullness.

It is a thrilling theme, depicting the discipline and the grace of God towards His people.

It is the writer's prayer and hope that new light will be shed, new aspects revealed, and new confidence established in the practical will of our God—namely, a holy people!

—MILTON S. AGNEW

Introduction

It is quite apparent to any student of the Word that holy living is desired by God in each of His children. It will be just as apparent that the full measure of this holiness is not achieved at the moment of spiritual birth. Certainly an element of holiness, if this be defined in its most simple terms as Godlikeness, is achieved at conversion. But all scripture and all the experience of man attest to the fact that the new convert must find an expansion of this first Godlikeness in the months and years to follow if he is to fulfill God's plan for him, if he is to fulfill his own hungers and his own newly awakened desires. There is more to the life of holiness than merely seeking a second crisis experience by the incoming of the Holy Spirit, though the latter is fundamental.

When and how this experience of sanctification may come upon a believer is a challenging and a rewarding study, worthy of the most searching examination of the Scriptures and of the experience of mankind.

1. The examination of the Word which we herewith present has certain characteristics. As a group of messages it deals with entire sections of scripture, from a single paragraph to an entire book. In this expository form the doctrine of holiness would be known to the Early Church generations before such doctrine would be examined as a systematic theology.

For example, Origen made possibly the first formal attempt toward a systematic theology in his *De Principiis,* written about A.D. 218. But this gave no adequate place, among other subjects, to the theology of either salvation or sanctification. Augustine (354-430), in his *Enchiridion*, presented the second formal attempt at a systematic theology. As an exposition of the creed the work was organized on the threefold Pauline principle of faith, hope, and love. What is considered by many as the first work worthy to be known as a systematic theology was *De Fide Orthodoxa*, a summary of the orthodox faith by John of Damascus, about A.D. 750. Thus can be seen the value of searching out the teaching which governed the Early Church of the first centuries, long before such teaching was organized into the systematic theology upon which the Church of today declares its creed and doctrine. Furthermore, that early teaching was established on extended passages of scripture, and not primarily on "proof texts." It was given in enlightening expository form, related to other doctrines and to the pressing needs of the believer—essays on holy living.

2. Again, the examination of the Word herewith presented is made in relationship to time, and thus to the progressive development of doctrine. Some care is herewith made to search the Scriptures in a chronological sequence, with an observation of the relationship of one passage of teaching to another, thus to see the fascinating development of the doctrine of New Testament holiness from the earliest teachings of our Lord himself, through the developing doctrine expounded by Paul and the writer of Hebrews, to those teachings registered in the latter part of the apostolic period by Peter and then by John.

A part of the fascination of this progressive study is to see, in the unfolding, a harmony of parts which, far from contradicting each other, complement each other in one element after another. In the light of this, an attempt is made in the final chapter to summarize these parts into a whole—a "systematic theology" if you please—of the doctrine of holiness and entire sanctification.

3. The examination of the Word undertaken in this study carries with it another aspect which is too seldom recognized, much less emphasized. This is a consideration of certain basic elements of the language in which the original manuscripts were written—Greek.

Unfortunately there are people, who, upon hearing the term *Greek,* are prone to close off their minds with a shrug, and the all-too-common phrase "It's all Greek to me."

But need this be? Let it be realized that the Greek of the New Testament was not a special "Holy Ghost" language, reserved for sainted mystics. Neither was it the classical Greek of that age, suited particularly to learned scholars. Rather, it was, as Dana and Mantey express it, "the ordinary colloquial tongue of the day, spoken throughout the Graeco-Roman world."[1] Because it was the natural, living language of the period, it was generally known as Koine or "common" Greek. It was to be found in such documents as receipts, wills, petitions, and private letters. And, since it was freely used and easily understood by the common people of that day who were neither theologians nor scholars, should we not assay to understand and profit by some basic facts and the intriguing wealth of the language—even though we may be neither mystics, scholars, nor theologians? Why should we remain unaware of nuances of truth contained in the Word which would be quite obvious to those of the Early Church?

For the statement "when the fulness of the time was come, God sent forth his Son" (KJV) refers not only to the fullness of time of prophecy, of world peace, of Roman roads which facilitated world travel, but also the fullness of time of the introduction of the most expressive language the world has known—the Greek language—in which to record the details of His "New Covenant."

For that reason there will be, from time to time, vocabulary observations regarding certain words which carry specific and exact meanings. On occasions this will be done by comparing various translations, sometimes by observing parallel usages of the word in the same translation.

Then there will also be, from time to time, an observation of the tense of verbs when this more clearly defines the thought being expressed. In the English, tense speaks of past, present, or future. However, in the Greek language, tense may mean not just the *time* of the action. It may also mean *kind* or *type* of action. The verb may declare either an event as a completed act, or a process as an extended action.

To illustrate this, note this statement from Dana and Mantey: "There are two fundamental ways of viewing action. It may be contemplated as a single perspective, as a point, which we may call *punctiliar* action; or it may be regarded as in progress, as a line, and this we may call *linear* action." The first is governed by the aorist tense, the latter by the present tense. The quotation continues: "The aorist may be represented by a dot (●), the present by a line (———)."[2] More details on this rule of Greek grammar will be found in the Appendix for the reader who is interested.

But it should become apparent that this *type* of action, known as the *aktionsart* (sort of action), can be very important in defining a specific statement such as a doctrine, or special truth. For example, considering the present tense of Matt. 7:7, it is translated by NASB: "*Keep asking*, and it shall be given to you; *keep seeking*, and you shall find; *keep knocking*, and it shall be opened to you" (margin). NEB correctly translates the aorist tense of 1 John 2:1 as: "But should anyone *commit a sin*"; and the present tense of 1 John 3:9 as "He cannot *be a sinner*, because he is God's child." (The italics in each illustration, as in all subsequent quotations, are mine.) This aspect of the Word will be frequently identified throughout this study.

It is with these three principles in mind that the reader is invited to examine the subsequent chapters of this book:

1. A group of scripture *messages* rather than isolated texts.

2. The *progressive development* of the doctrine of holiness.

3. The related aspects of *the Greek language*—the type of action *(aktionsart)* of Greek words and the exact meaning of Greek words.

It is with a profound hope of serving the cause of holiness and holy living that the materials contained herein were prepared. In a true sense we feel that they represent the "expository thoughts" of our Lord himself, and of holy men who built on the foundations laid by their Master. It has been our aim merely to expose and to elucidate *their* thoughts, not ours.

PART I:
What Jesus Said

1

*What Jesus said to His disciples
in His Sermon on the Mount concerning*

Christian Perfection

MATT. 5:21-48

It is striking that one of the early aspects of holy living, if not the earliest, to be enunciated by our Lord was that of Christian perfection. The account is listed by Matthew in the first part of Christ's basic instruction course to His recently chosen disciples. "Therefore you are to be perfect, as your heavenly Father is perfect" (Matt. 5:48).

Certainly holy living was to have a high standard. But perfection? This is viewed by many as visionary, as impractical, as entirely untenable. But Christ declared it. We must examine it thoroughly.

It is true, first of all, that this perfection related clearly to the area of love, as we will see. But Jesus also applied it to various commandments and rules of conduct, picked, it would seem, almost at random by Him from the multitude of commandments which at that time governed the Jewish community. It will become apparent, however, that this perfection was not necessarily that of *performance,* which is the outer obedience of action, but that of *purpose,* the inner obedience of the heart and the will. This is far more exacting. Furthermore, mankind was to be reminded that this perfection is to be in the sight of God, not of man. God knows our inmost thoughts and purposes and this makes the command the more awesome.

Christ's *final* teachings regarding holy living were dependent upon the coming of the Holy Spirit in His fullness. But this could not be at that time "because Jesus was not yet glorified" (John 7:39). Therefore it was not until His great high-priestly prayer of John 17 that Jesus disclosed in its depth and full significance His provision and plan for holy living. However, this early introduction to the standard of the divine plan for His people was to them as *startling* as it appeared to be *impossible.*

It was startling because God's children were not accustomed to being urged, much less commanded, to be perfect. It is true that Noah had been classified as "a just man and perfect in his generations" (Gen. 6:9, KJV), and that "when Abram was ninety years old and nine, the Lord appeared to Abram, and said unto him, I am the Almighty God; walk before me, and be thou perfect" (Gen. 17:1, KJV), and that the Levite of old received the admonition "Thou shalt be perfect with the Lord thy God" (Deut. 18:13, KJV). However, this was to a select few. This notion of complete goodness for *all* believers, *especially when it was to be compared to that of the Heavenly Father,* was startlingly new.

But our Lord was aiming at establishing the type of righteousness which would be worthy of the new dispensation of grace. God was dissatisfied with the "righteousness" which had been developed by the religious men of that day (v. 20): "For I say to you, that unless your righteousness surpasses that of the scribes and Pharisees, you shall not enter the kingdom of heaven." Or may we paraphrase this by substituting "the perfection" for the supplied word "that"? Thus we have: "Unless your righteousness surpasses *the perfection* [claimed by] the scribes and Pharisees . . ."

Note the interesting, and often commendable, standards of their "perfection" which Jesus chose, apparently at random, from numerous standards He might have listed—for they had many. "You shall not commit murder" (v. 21). Who can quarrel with that? "You shall not commit adultery" (v. 27). Certainly this is basic to any "perfection." "You shall not make false vows, but shall fulfill your vows to the Lord" (v. 33). This, too, surely is an intelligent approach to "perfection."

The next two however have an interesting "human" touch.

Pharisaic righteousness allowed a man to *be* a man. After all, even the holiest of men have personal rights! "An eye for an eye, and a tooth for a tooth" (v. 38). No man should be expected to be a doormat for the meannesses of others. Furthermore, this "perfection" of course included love toward your family, your fellow Israelite, your "neighbor," but it could not be expected to include enemies, or persecutors (v. 43)—of whom the Jew of that day had many. That would be asking too much.

But this type of righteousness was anathema to Jesus —and to their Heavenly Father. Its motive was wrong. It was practiced solely that they might be "noticed" by men (6:1), be "seen" by men (v. 5).

The righteousness that Jesus desired was not that of multiplied rules and laws, but of the spirit. The perfection He desired was not so much of performance as of purpose, not of accomplishment so much as of intent. The God Jesus represented—and the God He himself was—looks not on the outward appearance, but on the heart.

The "therefore" of the text reaches back into the previous paragraphs. Let's explore them, for in them are depicted several facets of this desired perfection.

1. This perfection first should be exhibited *in the spirit of reconciliation* rather than in the spirit of retalia-

tion. For retaliation harbors anger, and can even break out in murder.

> "You have heard that the ancients were told, 'You shall not commit murder;' and 'Whoever commits murder shall be liable to the court;' but I say to you that every one who is angry with his brother shall be guilty before the court; and whoever shall say to his brother, 'Raca,' shall be guilty before the supreme court; and whoever shall say, 'You fool,' shall be guilty enough to go into the hell of fire. If therefore you are presenting your offering at the altar, and there remember that your brother has something against you, leave your offering there before the altar, and go your way, first be reconciled to your brother, and then come and present your offering" *(Matt. 5:21-24)*.

There are two great passages which speak of our Heavenly Father's example to us of reconciliation rather than retaliation, of love rather than wrath, of life rather than death. These passages are both found in Paul's second group of Epistles, written 20 or 25 years later during his third missionary journey, and out of the maturity of his ministry.

> God . . . reconciled us to Himself through Christ, and gave us the ministry of reconciliation, namely, that God was in Christ reconciling the world to Himself, not counting their trespasses against them, and He has committed to us the word of reconciliation. Therefore, we are ambassadors for Christ, as though God were entreating through us; we beg you on behalf of Christ, be reconciled to God *(2 Cor. 5:18-20)*.

A few months later he wrote on the same subject, even more tenderly, "to all who are beloved of God in Rome":

> The love of God has been poured out within our hearts through the Holy Spirit who was given to us. For while we were still helpless, at the right time Christ died for the ungodly. For one will hardly die for a righteous man; though perhaps for the good man someone would dare even to die. But God demonstrates His own love toward us, in that while we were yet sinners, Christ

died for us. Much more then, having now been justified
by His blood, we shall be saved from the wrath of God
through Him. For if while we were enemies, we were
reconciled to God through the death of His Son, much
more, having been reconciled, we shall be saved by His
life. And not only this, but we also exult in God through
our Lord Jesus Christ, through whom we have now
received the reconciliation *(Rom. 5:5-11).*

Need more be said than Paul so eloquently has said?
We then echo Paul in repeating our Lord's admonition
that, in the spirit of reconciliation, "you are to be perfect,
as your heavenly Father is perfect"—in the spirit of reconciliation even toward him who has wronged you most,
regarding whom the "natural man" would be aroused to
anger, or even to murder. "To seventy times seven,"
declared Jesus, in the realm of forgiveness.

2. This Godlike perfection should be exhibited,
further, *in the spirit of self-discipline* rather than in the
spirit of self-indulgence—the self-indulgence which, in
man, leads to impurity of thought and deed.

"You have heard that it was said, 'YOU SHALL NOT
COMMIT ADULTERY;' but I say to you, that every one who
looks on a woman to lust for her has committed adultery
with her already in his heart. And if your right eye
makes you stumble, tear it out, and throw it from you;
for it is better for you that one of the parts of your body
perish, than for your whole body to be thrown into hell.
And if your right hand makes you stumble, cut it off,
and throw it from you; for it is better for you that one
of the parts of your body perish, than for your whole
body to go into hell" *(Matt. 5:27-30).*

And what is our Heavenly Father's example to us in
self-discipline? Possibly it is most graphically voiced by
Habakkuk when he exclaims of God, "Thou art of purer
eyes than to behold evil, and canst not look on iniquity"
(1:13, KJV). In a figurative sense, God has plucked out
His eye and thrown it from Him, that He might not even

contemplate sin. No wonder the seraphim cried out, "Holy, Holy, Holy, is the Lord of hosts" (Isa. 6:3); and the Psalmist (99:9) extolled, "Exalt the Lord our God, and worship at his holy hill; for the Lord our God is holy" (KJV). Indeed, "As your heavenly Father is perfect"—in dedication to that self-discipline which protects purity—"you are to be perfect." And how that discipline is needed *now!*

It has been suggested that the human mind is like a camera film. After exposure to an impure thought or suggestion it is possible to do one of two things, either to covet the thought and develop the plate, which fixes the picture permanently, or instantly to flood the plate with light, the Light of Jesus—then the picture is forever destroyed.

3. Again, this perfection should be *in the spirit of simplicity of language* rather than in the pompousness of speech which leads to excess and, in man, to perjury and to profanity.

> "Again, you have heard that the ancients were told, 'YOU SHALL NOT MAKE FALSE VOWS, BUT SHALL FULFILL YOUR VOWS TO THE LORD.' But I say to you, make no oath at all; either by heaven, for it is THE THRONE OF GOD; or by the earth, for it is the footstool of His feet; or by Jerusalem, for it is THE CITY OF THE GREAT KING. Nor shall you make an oath by your head, for you cannot make one hair white or black. But let your statement be, 'Yes, yes' or 'No, no;' and anything beyond these is of evil" *(Matt. 5:33-37).*

Man is tempted to a pretension, then to a carelessness of speech which, Jesus said, is unlike his Heavenly Father. Probably no passage of scripture can exceed, in its simplicity of language and in its economy of words, that greatest of legal passages, the Ten Commandments. These, in their totality, are encompassed in our English Bible within 15 verses. And the essence of the commandments is spoken in just 70 words. Now truly can Jesus then say, "As your heavenly Father is perfect"—in the spirit of simplicity of language and of sincerity of speech—"you [too] are to be perfect."

I recall vividly an experience at the University of Chicago, although nearly 50 years ago. The English professor, a gifted man, who also wrote a column in the *Chicago Daily News,* was given to profanity in the class. Every sentence or two contained a curse word. On a general assignment I ventured to write on "The Adequacy of the English Language."

I boldly protested that I had always been told that the use of profanity indicated one of two things: either laziness or an ignorance of the English language.

Unfortunately (?) I split an infinitive in the writing. The next day the professor fumed into class, soundly berating any man who "misused" the grammar criticizing another for profanity—and proceeded to read the entire essay to the class—split infinitive and all.

Of course I felt chagrined. But I was rather happy, too, that I had been "heard."

4. This perfection furthermore should exhibit itself *in a meek spirit of kindly response,* rather than in an aggressive spirit of grasping one's rights, of protecting personal dignity, of retribution and revenge.

> "You have heard that it was said, 'AN EYE FOR AN EYE, AND A TOOTH FOR A TOOTH.' But I say to you, do not resist him who is evil; but whoever slaps you on your right cheek, turn to him the other also. . . . And whoever shall force you to go one mile, go with him two. Give to him who asks of you, and do not turn away from him who wants to borrow from you" *(Matt. 5:38-42).*

It will be remembered that Jesus said, "He who has seen Me has seen the Father" (John 14:9); that Heb. 1:3 declares of Jesus and His Father, "He is the radiance of His glory and the exact representation of His nature." In that sense, then, we see the Father in His Son's response to specific circumstances. At His cruel trial Jesus may not actually have turned the other cheek, but He didn't strike back or curse. He did not resist evil men when they came to seize Him in the garden, nor did He snatch back His garment, nor refuse to walk the Via Dolorosa, nor even did He withhold His very life. And for these men He prayed, "Father forgive them."

Man needs to beware lest in claiming his rights he loses his witness.

There is a simple legend of a poor boy, the son of a widow, who had gathered from the woods a dish of strawberries. As he was returning home with his delicacy, a crusty old man saw his delectable treasure and startled him by calling out: "My lad, let me have your full dish and you take my empty one."

Pity for the old man's weakness and helplessness overcame the boy's reluctance to part with his berries. He made the exchange and then went back to the tedious task of again filling the empty dish.

Having accomplished this, he returned with it to his mother, to whom he told the story of his adventure. She examined the vessel, then exclaimed: "Ah, happy are we, my child. The dish is pure gold."

In this area of living, again Jesus can straightforwardly say, "As your heavenly Father is perfect" "you are [also] to be perfect"—in a meek spirit of kindly and gracious response.

Jesus might have spoken of many other aspects of perfection, such as respect for parents, for property, for the truth. But He chose to mention only one more.

5. This perfection should be exhibited *in the spirit of Christian love,* rather than in the spirit of classified favoritism.

"You have heard that it was said, 'YOU SHALL LOVE YOUR NEIGHBOR, AND HATE YOUR ENEMY.' But I say to you, love your enemies, and pray for those who persecute you; in order that you may be sons of your Father who is in heaven; for He causes His sun to rise on the evil and the good, and sends rain on the righteous and the unrighteous. For if you love those who love you, what reward have you? Do not even the tax gatherers do the same? And if you greet your brothers only, what do you more than others? Do not even the Gentiles do the same?" *(Matt. 5:43-47).*

As Jesus here declares, your Heavenly Father "causes His sun to rise on the evil and the good, and sends rain on the righteous and the unrighteous." God's impartiality is repeatedly declared (Rom. 2:11; Eph. 6:9; Col. 3:25), but Peter learned it in a striking revelation. God showed him by means of a vision of various foods lowered in a great sheet to the ground that "what God has cleansed, no longer consider unholy." In the midst of his perplexity as to what this might mean, he was summoned by Cornelius and went to his house. Then, opening his mouth, Peter said, "I most certainly understand now that God is not one to show partiality, but in every nation the man who fears Him and does what is right, is welcome to Him."

No wonder our Lord's disciples, too, are commanded to be impartial!

Furthermore, Jesus declared that God loved the *world* —all of it. And, again, He so expanded the definition of "neighbor" in His parable of the Good Samaritan that there was really now no room for an enemy.

Henry Ward Beecher is credited with saying: "Love is ownership. We own whom we love. The universe is God's because He loves it."

Thus, Jesus can urgently say, "As your heavenly Father is perfect"—in His all-encompassing love—in like fashion "you [too] are to be perfect."

It was during these same early months of His ministry

that Jesus pronounced one of the most lofty and definite sayings about God's nature which is to be found in the whole Bible. The second commandment had laid the foundations for this centuries before in declaring that no graven image could properly depict God. In condemning idolatry, the prophets during the centuries which intervened had been reinforcing this same principle. But it was left to Jesus to make the final announcement as a pinnacle in the progressive revelation of God which had continually mounted through the Old Testament.

> "But an hour is coming, and now is, when the true worshipers shall worship the Father in spirit and truth; for such people the Father seeks to be His worshipers. God is spirit; and those who worship Him must worship in spirit and truth" *(John 4:23-24)*.

God examines, not the outward form or act, but the *spirit* in which it is done. How true, "For God sees not as man sees, for man looks at the outward appearance, but the Lord looks at the heart" (1 Sam. 16:7).

Yes, Jesus was calling His own to perfection, to Christian perfection—not of outward appearance; not particularly of performance or accomplishment; not, if you please, to sinless perfection, or to Adamic perfection. Rather He was calling to a perfection of purpose, of intent, of spirit, and therefore also to a perfection of dedication, of surrender, of abdication of will. In this, indeed, the child of God may be expected to be perfect, as is his Heavenly Father.

As will become manifest, this godly perfection shall become the very foundation of true holy living.

Did not Charles Wesley catch something of this when he wrote the following verse?

> *In me Thine utmost mercy show,*
> *And make me like thyself below,*
> *Unblamable in grace;*

*Ready, prepared, and fitted here
By perfect holiness to appear
Before Thy glorious face.*

2

*What Jesus said to His disciples
during His Galilean ministry about*

The Discipline of the Cross

MATT. 16:24-28

Discipline as a requirement for Christian discipleship is not unique to this particular passage. During His Sermon on the Mount (Matthew 5) Jesus had recommended the tearing out of an eye, the cutting off and discarding of a right hand, if these members were a cause of sin. Again, he had demanded His disciples' first love (Matt. 10:37-38). Later on, He would, on seeing "great multitudes . . . going along with Him," appraise the cost of discipleship as including the "hating" of the members of the immediate family (Luke 14:26-31). But right now He was presenting a startling demand on those who chose to come after Him:

> Then Jesus said to His disciples, "If any one wishes to come after Me, let him deny himself, and take up his cross, and follow Me" *(Matt. 16:24).*

This was startling indeed for what it demanded, but more, because of the context in which it was stated.

Through incisive questioning Jesus had elicited Peter's notable confession: "Thou art the Christ, the Son of the living God." Upon this confession Christ had projected the building of His Church. In the strength of this memorable moment Jesus had then made His very first prediction of His death. Indeed, He commenced an entirely new area of teaching, announcing that He would "suffer many things . . . and be killed, and be raised up on the third day."

The response by Peter was probably an expression on behalf of all the disciples: "God forbid it, Lord! This shall never happen to You." Such a reprimand called forth possibly the sternest rebuke Jesus ever gave to any of His disciples, directed to Peter, but apparently including them all: "Get behind Me, Satan! You are a stumbling-block to Me; for you are not setting your mind on God's interests, but man's." How quickly had Peter changed from being a rock to being the tempter!

It was *then,* on the heels of this reprimand, that Jesus gave to His disciples the startling demand outlined in our text.

In the same manner that Jesus must die *for* sin, just so must His disciple die *to* sin, until, with Paul he can witness: "I have been crucified *with* Christ; and it is no longer I who live, but Christ lives in me; and the life which I now live in the flesh I live by faith in the Son of God, who loved me, and delivered Himself up for me" (Gal. 2:20); until he can agree with Paul's statement, "Knowing this, that our old self was crucified with Him, that our body of sin might be done away with, that we should no longer be slaves to sin" (Rom. 6:6).

1. Let us examine first the "self" designated by Jesus, then return to our text regarding the treatment of self.

By "self" Jesus did not mean the better self, the godly self, but rather the sinful self, that selfishness in which we were born because of Adam's sin. This selfishness produces all kinds of sins of the spirit, prevalent in the disciples when Jesus was with them, appearing among the believers of the Early Church, and persisting today among all too many Christians. Against these sins of the spirit the prophets of old had raised their voices, again and again, throughout the Old Testament.

Consider pride and arrogance. "Pride goes before destruction," declares Prov. 16:18, "and a haughty spirit before stumbling." While Mal. 4:1 declares, "'For behold, the day is coming, burning like a furnace; and all the arrogant and every evildoer will be chaff; and the day that is coming will set them ablaze,' says the Lord of hosts, 'so that it will leave them neither root nor branch.'"

Self-seeking is condemned in the name of the Lord in Jer. 45:5: "'But you, are you seeking great things for yourself? Do not seek them.'" And hear Obadiah speaking not only to Edom but to all who will exalt themselves unduly: "'Behold . . . the arrogance of your heart has deceived you . . . who say in your heart, "Who will bring me down to the earth?" Though you build high like the eagle, though you set your nest among the stars, from there I will bring you down,' declares the Lord" (2-4).

Isaiah, in 5:21, warns against conceit; "Woe to those who are wise in their own eyes, and clever in their own sight!" (See also Prov. 3:7.)

Envy and jealousy are often rebuked. "Fret not yourself because of evildoers, be not envious toward wrongdoers" (Ps. 37:1). "For . . . jealousy is as severe as Sheol; its flashes are flashes of fire, the very flame of the Lord" (Song of Sol. 8:6).

In like fashion the Old Testament pronounces judgment against worldly pleasure, anger, wrath, slander, falsehood, avarice, hypocrisy, strife.

All these sins of the spirit had beleaguered God's people through the centuries. Self had continued to express itself in countless ungodly traits and actions. *But it is not until this climactic moment in history that God can announce, in the person of His Son, a plan, not merely of condemnation OF sin by the Law, but of actual deliver-*

ance FROM sin through grace. Since the old self, in provision, has been crucified with Christ, such crucifixion is to be made actual in the believer by an act of faith, in a moment of surrender and self-crucifixion. Thus, as never before, the children of God now can be "more than conquerors through him that loved us" (Rom. 8:37, KJV). The believer can come to the place where Paul found himself when he declared: "I have been crucified with Christ . . . by faith in the Son of God, who loved me, and delivered Himself up for me."

As Paul later described it: "For what the Law could not do, weak as it was through the flesh, God did: sending His own Son in the likeness of sinful flesh and as an offering for sin, He condemned sin in the flesh, in order that *the requirement of the Law might be fulfilled in us,* who do not walk according to the flesh, but according to the Spirit" (Rom. 8:3-4).

The discipline of the cross for the believer could now be proclaimed, for the Son of God was even now facing the discipline of the cross, himself.

2. In the light of all this, let us now return to the text itself. To be a true disciple, a victorious Christian, certain things are required of the believer.

a. First, he must "deny himself." The verb *arneomai,* "to deny," has two aspects. It means "to say no," as in Matt. 26:70, "But he denied it before them all, saying, 'I do not know what you are talking about.'" (Also see Luke 8:45; Mark 14:70.) It also means "to refuse to acknowledge," "to disclaim," "to repudiate," as in Acts 3:14, "'But you disowned the Holy and Righteous One'"; and in Matt. 10:33, "'But whoever shall deny Me before men, I will also deny him before My Father.'" (Also see Acts 7:35; 2 Tim. 2:12.) Surely in our present text "deny" means to "say no" to the sinful self. But it also means "to disown," "to refuse to acknowledge," "to repudiate" such selfishness.

In this pattern Jesus cut squarely across the world's philosophy of life. For worldly success the motto must be "Assert yourself!" But for heavenly reward the words are "Deny yourself!" Now Jesus does not say that His follower is to deny himself of *something* in the way of a luxury, a pleasure, or even a habit; but he is to say no to *himself,* to refuse to acknowledge the claims of self. Indeed, self must die.

Now this denial of self is the hidden and internal act, while the taking up of the cross is the outward and external manifestation.

b. For, secondly, the one who wishes to come after Him must "take up his cross"—his own cross. And this speaks of the death of self, of self being crucified with Christ. It means to put oneself in the place of a condemned man on his way to crucifixion.

And how needful is this in order that "in all things he [Christ] might have the preeminence" (Col. 1:18, KJV). Indeed, unless self be slain, Christ cannot be manifest in His people. And the hour approaches when, on that day, "He comes to be glorified in His saints" (2 Thess. 1:10).

Leonardo da Vinci had just completed his masterpiece, "The Last Supper." He invited a friend to view and appraise it. The friend stood silently in awe. Then he exclaimed, "Those cups—what exquisite workmanship, what delicate color!" The great artist shot back, "I don't want you to see the cups. I want you to see the Christ." And with a stroke of his brush he wiped out the cups. There are no cups in Leonardo's "Last Supper." May there be no "self" in our portrayal of Christ.

Herbert Booth has well expressed it:

> *Within my heart, O Lord, fulfill*
> *The purpose of Thy death and pain,*

*That all may know Thou livest still
    In Blood-washed hearts to rule and reign.*

*O Lord, I gaze upon Thy face,
    That suffering face so marred for me.
Touched by the wonders of Thy grace,
    My heart in love goes out to Thee.*

*O Saviour, by Thy bleeding form
    The world is crucified to me;
Thy loving heart, so rent and torn,
    Thy suffering bids me share with Thee.*

Verse 25 of Matthew 16 modifies and enlarges the act of denial and crucifixion: "'For whoever wishes to save his life shall lose it; but whoever loses his life for My sake shall find it.'"

The large life comes through losing oneself in unselfish living for God. The higher self cannot live unless the lower self is nailed to the cross to die. Eternal life is born in the death of self.

The same truth is declared in John 12:25 even more plainly, in that there are used two words for "life," *psuchē*, life "in this world," the antonym of physical death; and *zoē*, life that is "eternal," the opposite of spiritual death. "'He who loves his [present] life loses it; and he who hates his [present] life in this world shall keep it to life eternal.'"

3. "And follow Me" is the third and final requirement. Only when we have denied self and taken up the cross are we ready to follow. There is no shortcut to discipleship.

It is interesting to note that the commands "deny" and "take" are in the aorist tense, but "follow" is in the continuous present tense. Denying oneself and taking of one's cross mark a crisis act, a spiritual "happening," while following is a lifetime procedure. (Note, in the Appendix, the significance of *Tense,* and particularly of the change of tenses.)

Thus, indeed, Christ was opening up a new dispensation of grace, not only for the forgiveness of sins, but also for victory over the very essence of sin in His believers. It is on the basis of this teaching that the messages of New Testament victorious living will be preached and written in the crucial years that follow, as recorded in Acts and the Epistles.

> *Oh, the bitter shame and sorrow*
> *That a time could ever be*
> *When I let the Saviour's pity*
> *Plead in vain, and proudly answered:*
> *All of self and none of Thee!*
>
> *Yet He found me; I beheld Him*
> *Bleeding on th' accursed tree,*
> *Heard Him pray: "Forgive them, Father!"*
> *And my wistful heart said faintly:*
> *Some of self and some of Thee!*
>
> *Day by day His tender mercy,*
> *Healing, helping, full and free,*
> *Sweet and strong and, ah, so patient,*
> *Brought me lower, while I whispered:*
> *Less of self and more of Thee!*
>
> *Higher than the highest heaven,*
> *Deeper than the deepest sea,*
> *Lord, Thy love at last has conquered;*
> *Grant me now my spirit's longing:*
> *None of self and all of Thee!*
>
> —THEODORE MONOD

3

What Jesus said to one of the scribes during His Passion Week concerning

Perfect Love

MARK 12:28-34

Although previously considered briefly in Christ's dissertation on Christian perfection in the Sermon on the Mount, the perfection of love in and by His followers is treated by Jesus much more fully at the very end of His public ministry. A running series of questions were thrown at Him by the Jewish rulers during Tuesday of His last week: a question about authority, another about taxes, a question about the resurrection, and, now, to end all questions, one about the commandments:

> And one of the scribes came and heard them arguing, and recognizing that He had answered them well, asked Him, "What commandment is the foremost of all?" *(Mark 12:28).*

This was not an unimportant question. The whole of the Jewish religious observance had come to depend on commandments. *To the extent that a man kept all the commandments he was a holy man.* But this had become an intolerable burden. For, by various means, the rabbis had compiled some 613 commandments—248 exhortations and 365 prohibitions. Some were "weighty" and some "light." And sorting laws into these categories caused endless dispute and disagreement. This scribe wanted, from

Jesus, His catalogue of classification. "What commandment is the foremost of all?" he challenges.

Now Matthew would make of this a capricious question by a scribe who hoped to embarrass Jesus: "And one of them, a lawyer, asked Him a question, *testing* Him." Mark would see in it a more kindly, a more sincere motive. This is evidenced both by the circumstances of the question ("recognizing that He had answered them well") and by the reply eventually elicited from the scribe, in his warm agreement with Jesus' answer, and in Jesus' commendation: "You are not far from the kingdom of God." But, whether capricious or sincere, the question itself was of importance to Jesus—and to His followers, both then and now.

If, in His wisdom, Jesus had singled out the "best" or the "most weighty" of the Ten Commandments, or of some other from among the 613 precepts revered by the rabbis, He could, for ages to come, have put His people under law and not under grace. That He respected the Law, however, is evident.

In the beginning of His ministry He had declared, "Whoever then annuls one of the least of these commandments, and so teaches others, shall be called least in the kingdom of heaven" (Matt. 5:19). He took opportunity on various occasions to restate this in greater depth, and to reinforce the Ten Commandments, which He knew and respected so well. In confronting and defeating the enemy at His temptation, Jesus quoted two prohibitions and one commandment from Moses (which may well have been from among the 613 precepts). Yes, Christ respected and enforced the laws and the commandments.

But the godliness that Christ was to proclaim and to expect was not to be one based on the restriction of the Law but on the motivation of love.

Quoting then from two Old Testament passages, He

referred His questioner first to the Shema, that passage which every pious Pharisee recited twice each day, found in Deut. 6:4-5, and then to a portion from Lev. 19:18:

> Jesus answered, "The foremost is, 'HEAR, O ISRAEL; THE LORD OUR GOD IS ONE LORD; AND YOU SHALL LOVE THE LORD YOUR GOD WITH ALL YOUR HEART, AND WITH ALL YOUR SOUL, AND WITH ALL YOUR MIND, AND WITH ALL YOUR STRENGTH.'
>
> "The second is this, 'YOU SHALL LOVE YOUR NEIGHBOR AS YOURSELF.' There is no other commandment greater than these" *(Mark 12:29-31).*

In this remarkable answer to the challenging question Jesus exhibits three unique and important aspects of the "kind" or classification of commandment which He would judge to be *the* great commandment.

1. The first aspect is that love, Christian love, *agape,* is the heart of this "foremost" commandment. Now only a God of love could make such a requirement. Elsewhere it is declared: "We love, because He first loved us" (1 John 4:19). The King James Version has inaccurately declared it, "We love *him,* because he first loved us." That is true, but incomplete. We can love Him, we can love others—indeed, we can love anybody with *agape* only because, with *agape,* He first loved us. And this, Jesus, as God's true Representative, clearly showed in all His own actions and attitudes.

This is the love that connotes concern, not coercion; compassion, and not compulsion. This is the love that recognizes a sense of value above a selfish personal feeling, a basic respect beyond human emotion. This is an unselfish, hetero-centered love which eschews personal gratification. It is the love which, not depending primarily on emotion, can be commanded and directed, and, therefore, the love for which man is responsible in the realm of his own volition.

In that sense "God so loved the world, that He gave His only begotten Son." In that sense Paul could say of the Son of God, He "loved me, and delivered Himself up for me." So, in that same sense, the individual Christian—for the verb "you shall love" is in the second person singular—is to love.

2. Another aspect of this "foremost" commandment is that this love is to reach two ways, toward God and toward man. It was as though Jesus had taken up and exhibited the two tablets of the Law—man's duty to God as it is written in the first four commandments on one side, and man's duty to fellowman as it is written in the remaining six commandments on the other side: (1) The sanctity of God's person: "You shall have no other gods before Me"; (2) The sanctity of God's image: "You shall not make for yourself an idol"; (3) The sanctity of God's name: "You shall not take the name of the Lord your God in vain"; (4) The sanctity of God's time: "Remember the sabbath day, to keep it holy"; (5) The sanctity of the home: "Honor your father and your mother"; (6) The sanctity of life: "You shall not murder"; (7) The sanctity of the person: "You shall not commit adultery"; (8) The sanctity of goods: "You shall not steal"; (9) The sanctity of the truth: "You shall not bear false witness"; (10) The sanctity of private possessions: "You shall not covet."

This love is to encompass all facets of life, both in heaven and in earth. Indeed, these two great areas of life are not to be separated. The one is as important as the other. For Jesus was herein giving the "great commandment" in two parts.

In a true sense the two areas cannot be separated. Love for God cannot be expressed fully or truly except through a similar love for man. Christian love for man cannot be rightly expressed except as an expression of one's love for God. There are those who have tried to separate them. A recluse has tried to focus his love solely on God, forgetting a needy and suffering world. A humanist has tried to care only for man, essentially forgetting the God who created man. Both have failed, and are bound to fail.

True Christianity must be a working relationship of the two parts of our Lord's "great" commandment.

True Christianity, furthermore, is a fulfillment of the entire old covenant as revealed in the new. In his account of this incident Matthew quotes Jesus as concluding, "On these two commandments depend ['hang,' KJV; 'are summed up,' Goodspeed; 'stem,' TLB] the whole Law and the Prophets." Someone has commented: "It was as though He said, 'Here are the two tablets of the Law. All else is commentary.'" Thus, Jesus is showing that the new covenant is in no way a contradiction or a correction of the old, but a fulfillment, a completion, a perfection. God did not change His mind or His character from the old to the new; He only revealed His unchanging character in its greater fullness. And God's children are the ones to demonstrate that truth to a world which hungers after such a God.

3. Another unique aspect of the kind of classification of the "first" commandment is its consuming quality. The love that God envisions demands the action of the whole personality. It would not be profitable to dwell at length on the fact that our text from Mark has four sources of our love, having added "mind" to the three in Deuteronomy, or on the fact that Matthew's account includes "mind" but omits "strength" or "might." What *is* important is to realize that this love is to be an expression of the total personality—the heart, the soul, the mind, the strength.

Neither is it important to dwell on the intriguing difference in the prepositions between Matthew and Mark.

The former says you must love *en* ("with," "by means of") your heart, soul, mind. The latter says *ex* ("from," "out of") the depths, the inexhaustible resources of these parts of your life you shall love. Actually they complement one another in discovering the depth of the resources of that love.

What *is* important is the recurrent word "all." God calls for no partial devotion. It is to be from all the heart, all the soul, all the mind, all the strength. Halford E. Luccock has written: "When we give to God a mere fraction of ourselves, God himself becomes a mere fraction of what he might be to us. Implicit in these words is Christ's revelation of the nature of God. Only a God who is love would make love his supreme demand."[1]

Furthermore, this godly love is toward our neighbor. And our neighbor is every man. Not the man of our own family, of our own race, of our own pattern of life. But every man is the child of our Heavenly Father, for every man is of priceless value in the eyes of our Father. This love is consuming in that it will extend to *every* man, without exceptions.

Love thus becomes less a single action than a life, less a precept than a baptism.

It is thus that the life of holiness can be called "perfect love," and the experience of entire sanctification can be called "a baptism of love." Truly the disciples experienced this on the Day of Pentecost. The throng which they had contemplated with abject fear they suddenly devoured with love. The man at the gate Beautiful whom they had ignored suddenly became an object of great compassion and concern. John, who had been known as one of the "Sons of thunder" (Mark 3:17) and who had been one of those desiring to call fire down on the opposing Samaritans (Luke 9:54), became known as the apostle of love.

The testimony of Samuel L. Brengle, well-known and

powerful exponent of holiness, is worth noting. In his book *Helps to Holiness,* Brengle, in speaking about his sanctification, said:

> But God meant greater things for me. On the following Tuesday morning, just after rising, with a heart full of eager desire for God, I read these words of Jesus at the grave of Lazarus: "I am the resurrection and the Life. He that believeth on Me, though he were dead, yet shall he live, and he that liveth and believeth on Me shall never die. Believest thou this?" The Holy Ghost, the other "Comforter," was in those words, and in an instant my soul melted before the Lord like wax before fire, and I knew Jesus. He was revealed in me as He had promised, and I loved Him with an unutterable love. I wept and adored, and loved and loved and loved. I walked out over Boston Common before breakfast, and still wept and adored and loved. Talk about the occupation of Heaven! I do not know what it will be—although, of course, it will be suited to, and commensurate with, our redeemed capacities and powers; but this I then knew, that if I could lie prostrate at the feet of Jesus to all eternity and love and adore Him, I would be satisfied—satisfied—satisfied![2]

Certainly, the Lord intended nothing less for any of His people. Perfect love has been and can be the experience of any. And it was on this presentation of that perfect love that the early men of God built their own experience. It then became the basis of the holy writings upon which men have formulated our theology.

The hymnal, in its vast wealth of songs regarding perfect love, reflects this doctrine, and is worthy of a brief examination.

Charles Wesley has numerous hymns on the subject, among them:

> *Wrestling on in mighty prayer,*
> *Lord, we will not let Thee go*
> *Till Thou all Thy mind declare,*
> *All Thy grace on us bestow;*

> *Peace, the seal of sin forgiven,*
> *   Joy, and perfect love impart;*
> *Present everlasting heaven,*
> *   All Thou hast and all Thou art.*

* * *

> *The whole of sin's disease,*
> *   Spirit of health, remove,*
> *Spirit of perfect holiness,*
> *   Spirit of perfect love.*

> *Hear my pleading, Lord;*
> *   Make my spirit free.*
> *Fill my soul with perfect love;*
> *   Oh, come and dwell in me!*

William Booth has given us:

> *O Christ of pure and perfect love,*
> *   Look on this sin-stained heart of mine!*
> *I thirst Thy cleansing grace to prove;*
> *   I want my life to be like Thine.*
> *Oh, see me at Thy footstool bow,*
> *And come and sanctify me now!*

> *Oh, pour on me the cleansing flood,*
> *   Nor let Thy side be cleft in vain!*
> *'Tis done, I feel the precious Blood*
> *   Does purge and keep from every stain.*
> *To all the world I dare avow*
> *That Jesus sanctifies me now.*

William Hutchins has written in the same spirit of searching and expectation:

> *While here before Thy cross I kneel,*
> *   To me Thy love impart;*
> *With a deep burning love for souls,*
> *   Lord, fill my craving heart.*

Deepen in me Thy work of grace;
  Teach me to do Thy will;
Help me to live a spotless life,
  Thy holy laws fulfill.

Lord, fill my craving heart
  With a deep, burning love for souls,
Lord, fill my craving heart.

4

*What Jesus said to His disciples
during the final hours of His ministry about*

The Paraclete

JOHN 14—16

Our Lord's words regarding the Holy Spirit are central, and of vital importance in laying the foundation for any doctrine of holy living. Jesus speaks of Him as "the Comforter," which, from the Greek, is the Paraclete.

The well-known "Paraclete Sayings" are contained in three chapters of John, expressing the heart of Christ's teaching on the subject. But, first, we must give brief attention to His other teachings on this subject in scattered areas of the Gospels.

Probably our Lord's first reference is in His acknowledgment of His own enduement of the Holy Spirit with power at the time of His baptism. The words were spoken to His own townspeople at a Nazareth synagogue service on a Sabbath day, immediately following His temptation.

> And Jesus returned to Galilee in the power of the Spirit; and news about Him spread through all the surrounding district. And He began teaching in their synagogues and was praised by all. And He came to Nazareth, where He had been brought up; and as was His custom, He entered the synagogue on the Sabbath, and stood up to read. And the book of the prophet Isaiah was handed to Him. And He opened the book, and found the place where it was written,

"The Spirit of the Lord is upon Me,
Because He anointed Me to preach the gospel to the poor.
He has sent Me to proclaim release to the captives,
And recovery of sight to the blind,
To set free those who are downtrodden,
To proclaim the favorable year of the Lord."

And He closed the book and gave it back to the attendant, and sat down; and the eyes of all in the synagogue were fixed upon Him. And He began to say to them, "Today this Scripture has been fulfilled in your hearing" *(Luke 4:14-21)*.

The example of this to Christians as "the firstfruits of the Spirit" must be of great importance. Peter later declared: "You know of Jesus of Nazareth, how God anointed Him with the Holy Spirit and with power, and how He went about doing good, and healing all who were oppressed by the devil; for God was with Him" (Acts 10:38).

Immediately following this, during His earliest ministry, our Lord made two deeply significant statements about the Holy Spirit, one regarding His ministry, and the other regarding the very nature of God and of the worship He now expected in this new dispensation. The first was given to Nicodemus; the second, to the woman at the well —recorded in John 3:5-6 and 4:23-24 respectively. The first speaks of regeneration, the beginning of Christian life; the second, of worship, the cultivation of the Christian life.

Jesus answered, "Truly, truly, I say to you, unless one is born of water and the Spirit, he cannot enter into the kingdom of God. That which is born of the flesh is flesh; and that which is born of the Spirit is spirit" *(John 3:5-6)*.

"An hour is coming, and now is, when the true worshipers shall worship the Father in spirit and truth; for such people the Father seeks to be His worshipers. God is spirit; and those who worship Him must worship in spirit and truth" *(John 4:23-24)*.

Again, during His Galilean ministry, Jesus found occasion to warn the scribes and Pharisees sternly against blasphemy against the Holy Spirit (Matt. 12:31-32; Mark 3:28-29).

It was toward the end of His ministry that He made two other significant pronouncements. The first came out of a frank request made by one of His disciples after beholding Jesus in prayer: "Lord, teach us to pray just as John also taught his disciples." To this He responded by the well-known "Lord's Prayer," with His parable of the importunate friend; and then, as the climax, of how a father will respond to the request of his child, Jesus gave the profound, if astonishing, assurance: "If you then, being evil, know how to give good gifts to your children, how much more shall your Heavenly Father give the Holy Spirit *to those who ask Him?*" To the disciples this must indeed have been astounding, for this is the *first* occasion recorded of the Holy Spirit being actually *offered* to anyone *in answer to prayer*. It would pave the way for the more precise statements regarding the Paraclete, made a few weeks later.

The second was less a pronouncement than an inference, interpreted by John when he recorded it many decades later, but again preparing the way for the advent of the Spirit in His fullness.

It was during this same period of our Lord's ministry, whether just after or before, that Jesus was in attendance at Jerusalem at the Feast of Tabernacles. John records the event in 7:37-39 as follows:

> Now on the last day, the great day of the feast, Jesus stood and cried out, saying, "If any man is thirsty, let him come to Me and drink. He who believes in Me, as the Scripture said, 'From his innermost being shall flow rivers of living water.'" But this He spoke of the Spirit, whom those who believed in Him were to

receive; for the Spirit was not yet given, because Jesus was not yet glorified.

Undoubtedly, these introductory areas of teaching by Jesus regarding the Holy Spirit—His part in the Christian's spiritual birth, His part in Christian worship, His divine nature which accepts not blasphemy, His availability to those who request Him, and His promised outpouring after Jesus was glorified—these would prepare the disciples for the more explicit proclamations regarding the Paraclete.

Now the Greek word *paraclētos* is used four times for the Holy Spirit in John 14; 15; and 16 (where it is translated "Comforter" in the KJV), and once when referring to Jesus as "Advocate" in 1 John 2:1. The word is variously translated when referring to the Holy Spirit as "Helper," "Advocate," "Counsellor," and, when referring to Jesus, as "Advocate," "Helper," "One who pleads our cause," "Intercessor," "Someone to stand by you."

It literally means "one called alongside." When speaking of a friend of the accused person in court, it indicated an advocate, a pleader, an intercessor. Referring to the Holy Spirit, the word was intended to mean that He can be called to our side, both to give strength and courage to meet the demands of life, and also to plead our cause as an Advocate, a Counsellor. On the other hand, Jesus has been "called to the side of God," *there* to be our Intercessor, our Advocate, One who pleads our cause. Thus believers have a Paraclete with them on earth, and a Paraclete with God in heaven.

What is obvious is that there is not one English word precisely and exactly conveying the meaning of the Greek word *paraclētos*. Probably the title "Paraclete" is the most meaningful for the Holy Spirit, and possibly "Advocate" for Jesus.

We look now to the "Paraclete Sayings." There are

five of them if the last two are separated; four if you combine them, as we will. These sayings were part of our Lord's last discourse with His disciples on the very eve of His crucifixion.

1. In the midst of a conference centered on assuring His disciples, Jesus turned to them with:

"If you love Me, you will keep My commandments. And I will ask the Father, and He will give you another Helper, that He may be with you forever; that is the Spirit of truth, whom the world cannot receive, because it does not behold Him or know Him, but you know Him because He abides with you, and will be in you. I will not leave you orphans; I will come to you" *(John 14:15-18).*

Although Jesus had previously invited His disciples to pray for the Holy Spirit, this, in truth, is the first time the Holy Spirit is mentioned as Christ's *special Gift* to His people. He, the Spirit, would be a Stranger to the world, unseen, unknown, rejected. But He is the token of difference between the believer and the unbeliever. His presence marks the true Christian. All Christians *possess* the Holy Spirit (Rom. 8:9). The difference, however, between *with* you and *in* you is significant; for it indicates that, while the Spirit was present, watching over the disciples at the time, a crisis moment was coming when the Spirit would enter *into* the lives of the disciples, *possessing them,* and controlling them from within. Such an experience had not yet been theirs; it came on the Day of Pentecost.

Although the promise "I will not leave you orphans; I will come to you," is interpreted by some to apply to His appearances after the Resurrection, and by others to His second coming, the most likely meaning appears to be that He would come to them *in His Spirit.* Although He was leaving them physically, He would *never* leave them spiritually. This is in line with His promise, "Lo, I am with you always, even to the end of the age" (Matt. 28:20).

2. The second "Paraclete Saying" is a continuation of the same discourse, identifying the Paraclete as Teacher and Reminder. These were areas where the disciples would have profound needs—the need to understand and the need to recall. For theirs was to be the task of recording the facts and the sayings of Jesus' life, and of comprehending the great truths so that, through their own preaching and writing, they might accurately express an interpretation and an enlargement of His sayings and doctrines.

> "These things I have spoken to you, while abiding with you. But the Helper, the Holy Spirit, whom the Father will send in My name, He will teach you all things, and bring to your remembrance all that I said to you" *(John 14:25-26)*.

3. It was at the end of a conference on relationships (John 15)—their relationship to Him as the True Vine, to each other in love, to the world in its hatred—that He gave the third "Paraclete Saying." It had to do with their relationship to the Paraclete as co-witnesses with Him to Christ. In a sense it foreshadowed Acts 1:8.

> "When the Helper comes, whom I will send to you from the Father, that is the Spirit of truth, who proceeds from the Father, He will bear witness of Me, and you will bear witness also, because you have been with Me from the beginning" *(John 15:26-27)*.

There are many ways the Holy Spirit would bear witness to Christ after coming to them—in miracles, in inspired preaching, by rebuking blasphemy, through enlightening the believers, in guiding the Church, by cleansing from sin. And it was in cooperation with the Paraclete, as He possessed their lives, that the disciples became the irrefutable witnesses that they were in the story of the

Church as given in Acts. Jesus well knew the absolute need of a Spirit-filled life for effective witnessing.

4. The final "Paraclete Saying" comes in the midst of a conference on revelation in chapter 16 with which Jesus concluded His highly important and instructive series in those final hours with His men.

A little chorus was undoubtedly born from this:

When He has come to you,
Souls will be won
And revivals begun,
When He has come to you.

"It is [actually] to your advantage that I go away," Jesus was telling them, so that the Holy Spirit could come. And when He is come to you, He will affect action in three areas: He will convict the world, guide you as disciples, and glorify Me, the Christ.

> "But I tell you the truth, it is to your advantage that I go away; for if I do not go away, the Helper shall not come to you; but if I go, I will send Him to you. And He, when He comes, will convict the world concerning sin, and righteousness, and judgment; concerning sin, because they do not believe in Me; and concerning righteousness, because I go to the Father, and you no longer behold Me; and concerning judgment, because the ruler of this world has been judged.
>
> "I have many more things to say to you, but you cannot bear them now. But when He, the Spirit of truth, comes, He will guide you into all truth; for He will not speak on His own initiative, but whatever He hears, He will speak; and He will disclose to you what is to come.
>
> "He shall glorify Me; for He shall take of Mine, and shall disclose it to you. All things that the Father has are Mine; therefore I said, that He takes of Mine, and will disclose it to you" *(John 16:7-15).*

The key to this was to be the events of Pentecost. The disciples were not yet ready after three years with their

Master; they would not be ready after Calvary; they would not even be ready on the day of the open tomb, or on the day of His ascension. But "I will send Him *to you.* And . . . when He comes [to you, He] will . . ." The Holy Spirit would work primarily through Spirit-filled men, through people, through flesh and blood.

a. The world will be *convicted;* convicted of sin, the basic sin of unbelief. However, note the phrase more carefully: "because they do not believe *in* Me." Now this faith is not passive, acquiescent, innocuous. It is active, aggressive, penetrating. The preposition actually is *into.* The Greek language looks at the act of believing in a different way from the English; it thinks in terms of putting one's faith *into* someone. Saving faith is a *penetrating* faith.

The same Greek words are used of Jesus regarding men: "But Jesus did not *commit* himself *unto* them" (John 2:24, KJV). He was not entrusting himself into their hands. Thus the world does not *entrust* or *commit* itself *into* His care, as is required in John 3:16. Of this rejection the Holy Spirit will convict the world.

The world will be convicted also concerning righteousness: "because I go to the Father, and you no longer behold Me." It was in His resurrection as a final victory over sin and in His ascension that the perfect righteousness of Christ was finally shown. In the light of that, the world will stand convicted of its own sinfulness, its own ungodliness, but also of its own possibilities of righteousness.

The world will also be convicted "concerning judgment, because the ruler of this world has been judged." Jesus, at the Cross, and through the empty tomb, defeated Satan, so that he stands already judged. In that fact, the world will stand convinced and convicted regarding a judgment to come for all mankind.

Conviction? This descended upon the multitudes unto

repentance and salvation after that the Holy Spirit was come upon the disciples.

Conviction, repentance, regeneration—again these will come unto the world in the same ratio that God's people are possessed by the Holy Spirit. His task, His methods, His channels of operation have not changed.

b. But as to the disciples, when the Paraclete is come to them they will, in contrast, be *guided.* For many months Jesus had been saying "many things" to them. There were yet "many more things" to be said. Through the indwelling Spirit they would be guided "into all the truth"; as if specially meaning, "I am *the* Truth. Into all of the truth concerning Me you will be guided." And this will be by the Spirit passing on to the disciples the contents of heavenly councils. "He will not speak on His own initiative, but whatever He hears, He will speak." What an access to the Truth!

c. And, as for the Lord himself, He will be *glorified.* When the Paraclete has come to the disciples, "He shall glorify Me," says Jesus. He will continually teach and disclose and guide disciples to edify Christ. Any religious teaching which does not exalt Christ has a fatal defect about it. It cannot be of the Spirit.

Let us now summarize His Paraclete teachings apart from this concentrated area in John's Gospel.

It was Luke (24:49) who recalls our Lord's final charge to the disciples: "And behold, I am sending forth *the promise of My Father* upon you: but you are to stay in the city until you are clothed with power from on high."

It was Luke again who recorded our Lord's charge to His disciples regarding their baptism to come:

> And gathering them together, He commanded them not to leave Jerusalem, but to wait for *what the Father had promised,* "Which," He said, "you heard of from Me; for John baptized with water, but you shall be

baptized with the Holy Spirit not many days from now" *(Acts 1:4-5).*

Of this "promise of the Father," namely, the baptism of the Holy Spirit, Ralph Earle in commenting on Mark 1:1-13 observes:

In view of the clear assertion of John the Baptist here it is difficult to understand the almost universal neglect in the Christian church of the baptism with the Holy Spirit. Water baptism is not a *Christian* rite. The only distinctive and utterly unique Christian baptism is the baptism with the Holy Spirit. That cannot be duplicated by any other religion. It is peculiarly Christ's: "*He* shall baptize you with the Holy Spirit."[1]

And, finally, it is again Luke who records the remainder of our Lord's last conversation with the disciples —which pertains to their relationship to the Holy Spirit:

And so when they had come together, they were asking Him, saying, "Lord, is it at this time You are restoring the kingdom to Israel?" He said to them, "It is not for you to know times or epochs which the Father has fixed by His own authority; but you shall receive power when the Holy Spirit has come upon you; and you shall be My witnesses both in Jerusalem, and in all Judea and Samaria, and even to the remotest part of the earth" *(Acts 1:6-8).*

Our Lord's thoughts regarding the Paraclete were directed to His disciples, and fulfilled at Pentecost. But can we doubt that *any one* of them is not applicable to believers of all time, including today? Let us recall that our Lord, in His final great prayer, said: "I ask on their behalf; I do not ask on behalf of the world, but of those whom Thou hast given Me; for they are Thine." Later He prayed, "Sanctify them in the truth. . . . I do not ask in behalf of these alone, but *for those also who believe in Me through their word"* (John 17:9, 17, 20).

It will be in the light of these memories and this conviction that we will hear the disciples, again and again, expounding to their churches, to their converts, to believers of all lands and of all generations these same wonderful truths regarding the Paraclete.

Holy Ghost, we bid Thee welcome;
　Source of life and power Thou art.
Promise of our Heavenly Father,
　Now thrice welcome in our heart.

Come like dew from heaven falling;
　Come like spring's refreshing shower.
Holy Ghost, for Thee we're calling;
　Come in all Thy quickening power.

Hearts are open to receive Thee,
　Though we've grieved Thee o'er and o'er.
Holy Ghost, we greatly need Thee;
　Come, abide forevermore.
　　　　　　—Mrs. C. H. Morris

5

What Jesus said in His high-priestly prayer for His disciples—of yesterday and today

Sanctify Them

JOHN 17

Jesus, who can "sympathize with our weaknesses" in that He "has been tempted in all things as we are, yet without sin" (Heb. 4:15), himself gave an example of practical holiness in everyday living. It is not surprising then that He also gave admonition to and that He made provision for victorious living among His people.

Throughout His teaching He made plain God's plan for holy living. The Beatitudes are an illustration in point. A humble poverty of spirit, meekness, a passionate searching for righteousness, purity of heart—are these not all qualities of a holy man? His interpretation of Old Testament law, as given in that same fifth chapter of Matthew, likewise set the standard for holy living. Hatred is murder; a lustful looking after a woman is adultery; divorce, except for unfaithfulness, is forbidden; an avoidance of the full truth is perjury. Sin lies not just in the act, but more in the intent, the spirit, the uncontrolled desire. These standards of uncompromising righteousness identified and permeated all His teaching.

Furthermore, Jesus declared that He came into the world "that they might have life, and might have it abundantly" (John 10:10). Paul recognized this twofold purpose in his letters. To Timothy he wrote, "It is a trustworthy statement, deserving full acceptance, that Christ Jesus came into the world *to save sinners,* among whom I am foremost of all" (1 Tim. 1:15); to the Ephesians: "Christ also loved *the church,* and gave Himself up for her; *that He might sanctify her,* having cleansed her by the washing of water with the word . . . that she should be holy and blameless" (5:25-27).

It is not surprising then that Jesus enunciated, as the very heart of His great high-priestly prayer, the petition, "Sanctify them."

But, for the sake of inclusiveness, let us look, at least in a cursory fashion, at this entire chapter—the outpouring of a great heart in our Lord's "last will and testament" for His disciples. Remember that this was the climax of a moving and deeply significant evening. It was the last He would spend before His passion, and He had been in close conference with His disciples. He now brings us into the very sanctuary of His heart.

He opened His conversation with His Father with reference to himself, with a petition and with a report—a petition that His glory might be returned to Him, so that in turn He might glorify the Father and also be the Dispenser of eternal life; a report that in a real sense He had already glorified His Father in that He had now accomplished the work God had given Him to do. He had made God's name manifest, and He had given out "the words" provided by God.

He was now ready to make intercession for those present whom God had given Him (v. 9), but also for those myriads of others, through the ages, who, though not present, would come to believe on Him "through their word" (v. 20). This inclusiveness is of vital importance. Jesus was praying for His *great* family, not just for 11 men who were with Him at the moment, but for all believers everywhere, for all time. That included you; it included me.

Now it is not surprising that the prayer does not follow a structured order. It is not an organized discourse. Rather it is the fervent outpouring of a burning heart. Yet, having said that, there is relevance, there is progression. The main thrust and driving theme appears to be "Keep them." And is that surprising? He was leaving 11 men—the twelfth He had already "lost"—just 11 men to proclaim this revolutionary new covenant. And these were men with demonstrated frailties, doubts, differences. The success of His entire mission rested upon them. And those who would believe through their word would be men "of like passions," of like frailties, of like human limitations. Thus, for their own spiritual life, and for the very propagation of the gospel, they must be kept.

Note that it was through their claiming of the several aspects He here enunciates that the Early Church exploded into the world as a bomb from eternity. And whenever the later Church neglected them, it withered and all but died. Indeed, these are the divinely provided privileges which, as they are claimed, will today again propel the Church and the gospel into a needy world. Well, then, may we take heed to them—as individuals, and as the Church of Christ.

He prayed that His people might be kept—kept in unity (v. 11), kept in joy (v. 13), kept from evil (v. 15), kept through sanctification (v. 17), kept as a glorious Church (v. 22).

1. "Keep them . . . that they may be one, *even as We are*" (v. 11) is repeated in verses 21, 22, 23. The basis of this oneness is the Shema. Deut. 6:4, known and daily repeated by every good Jew, reads, "Hear, O Israel: The Lord our God is one Lord" (KJV). This is the Shema. As

there are no schisms or divisiveness in the Godhead, so there must be none among the believers.

But "that they may be one" *what?* Jesus did not mean that all Christians should have the same personality. The adjective "one" is not masculine in gender. Personalities, under Christ's influence, may be refined but not regimented. Certainly this proved true among His disciples, who retained their rugged individualism and personality differences in the Early Church. They did not all become flamboyant Peters, nor contemplative Matthews, nor questioning Thomases. They were themselves.

Neither can this be a plea for a super Church. "One" is not feminine in gender to agree with *ekklesia*. Rather the adjective "one" is neuter. It might well be matched with the neuter *pneuma,* "spirit," one spirit. For this certainly characterized the Early Church and marks the true Church of today. The neuter "one" might well be matched with *sōma,* "body." 1 Cor. 12:12 declares that the body is "one and yet has many members," members who "have the same care for one another," the body of which Christ is the Head (Col. 1:18).

This oneness may also well be matched with the unique Greek word *homothumadon,* which, appearing first in Acts 1:14, is essentially unique to the Book of Acts, and knits it together with its constant repetition (1:14; 2:1, 46; 4:24; 15:25; etc.). It is a word of strength, which the KJV aptly translates "with one accord." It is a combination of *homou,* "together" or "side by side," as in John 20:4, and of *thumos,* "a strong passion of the mind." Thus: "a-strong-together-passion-of-the-mind." This was the Church at its aggressive best.

2. Jesus also prayed that they might be kept in joy, a full joy, His joy (v. 13). The Pharisees—and many others, no doubt—had presented religion as a sorrowful, unhappy,

burdensome—indeed, repulsive—experience, for young and old alike. "Keep them joyful" was Christ's earnest petition—the joy of fulfilled purpose (Heb. 12:2); the joy of fruitful living and abiding love (John 15:11); the joy of the angels in heaven (Luke 15:10).

That this joy was fulfilled in the Early Church is characterized by such a passage as Acts 2:41-47, which, after describing the continual fruitfulness of the Church's ministry, concludes:

> And day by day continuing with one mind *[homothumadon]* in the temple, and breaking bread from house to house, they were taking their meals together with gladness and sincerity of heart, praising God, and having favor with all the people. And the Lord was adding to their number day by day those who were being saved.

How fortunate the Christian, how fortunate the church, which keeps paramount "the joy of the Lord"! It needs greater expression, however, in our lives and in our services.

One of the things which has made the Salvation Army attractive through the years has been the joy expressed in its services. A Salvationist of the early 1880s, James Bateman, composed the following words to the tune of a popular song of the day:

Come shout and sing, make heaven ring
  With praises to our King,
Who bled and died, was crucified,
  That He might pardon bring.
His blood doth save the soul
Doth cleanse and make it whole,
The blood of Jesus cleanses white as snow.

Oh, the blood of Jesus cleanses white as snow;
Yes, I know!

*I bless the happy day when He washed my sins
   away,
The blood of Jesus cleanses white as snow.*

This and other such rollicking songs are still sung with abandon, hand clapping, the beat of the drum, and with a not occasional "Hallelujah!" But a note of warning should be added that, except the singing of these songs be accompanied by the other qualities Jesus prayed would characterize His Church, it can indeed become as "a noisy gong or a clanging cymbal." It must be *His* joy.

3. Our Lord progresses with His prayer. "Keep them from the evil one" (v. 15), or, as the KJV says, "from the evil." In either case Jesus knew only too vividly the encompassing power of sin, transgression, wickedness—whether as an act or as embodied in a person. Evil would contaminate His men, destroy His Church. There could be no compromise.

This preservation could not be accomplished, however, by taking them out of the world. On three occasions there is recorded God's man praying that he be removed from the world. Moses in his extremity (Num. 11:15) cried, "Kill me"; Elijah saw himself as the only godly person left and pled "that he might die" (1 Kings 19:4); while Jonah (4:3, 8) despaired of God's goodness and requested, "Take my life." None of these prayers was answered. *God's plan is not that His men be removed out of the world, but that the world should be kept out of His men.* Water and a boat belong together. But the boat should be kept in the water and not the water in the boat. Christ's men and the world belong together, but in the same relationship. The men should be in the world, but the world should not be in the men. Our Lord was avoiding the dual pitfalls of worldliness and monasticism. He still is.

A portion of this generation (too large a portion) both

young and old is disenchanted with the Church today. It sees the Church either as too "exalted" to care, to understand, and to be realistic; or as too "worldly" to challenge, to have the answer to today's needs, and to offer any redemptive power. But this generation still responds to the church, to the Christian, that is *in* this world, but not *of* it. Jesus knew what He was saying!

4. The Lord now expresses His central request, "Sanctify them in the truth" (v. 17). But this request attains new urgency. He dares use the imperative mood, literally to command His Father, "You really must sanctify them in the truth." Furthermore, He does not ask that they be "justified," be "saved," for they already were His —and God's (vv. 6-12). They were justified; they were saved; they were regenerate; they were His. He had previously told His disciples (Luke 10:20): "Nevertheless do not rejoice in this, that the spirits are subject to you, but rejoice that your names are recorded in heaven." *They did not need to be saved, but they did need to be sanctified.* Thus He directs this prayer, not "on behalf of the world" (the ungodly, the unsaved), "but of those whom Thou hast given Me."

But that is not all. See verse 20: "I do not ask in behalf of these alone, but for those also who believe in Me through their word" (the children of God, the saved, the justified of all time—us). There are those who make of the Pentecostal event a sign only for the Early Church, for those then living. This undoubtedly is true as far as outward signs and wonders are concerned. But it is not true as far as the sanctification of individual lives is concerned. We may well pray: "Do it again, Lord; do it again."

The verb *hagiadzo,* here translated "sanctify," has two aspects. The first is to separate from the *commonplace,* to "consecrate," to "dedicate." The other is to separate from the *unclean,* the *unholy,* to "sanctify." The first usage is infrequent. Matt. 23:17, 19 refers to the consecration of the gold by the Temple and the offering by the altar. John 10:36 speaks of Jesus as "Him, whom the Father sanctified [consecrated] and sent into the world." And here Jesus declares, "And for their sakes I sanctify [dedicate] Myself." Now dedication asks for no change in character, only a change in purpose. *Consecrate* and *dedicate* are synonyms, meaning to set apart or devote to a sacred purpose. Any book of synonyms will show that they are synonymous with each other, but *not* with *sanctify.*

The second usage of *hagiadzo* is to "sanctify"—the translation correctly given elsewhere in the New Testament. *In contrast to dedication, sanctification changes the character* of the person. Furthermore, *man* can dedicate, consecrate, but only *God* can sanctify, make holy. It is in this last sense that Jesus declared, "Sanctify them through the truth."

Unfortunately there is confusion with certain translations, notably the NEB, in that in this text, and elsewhere, the word is given as "dedicate" or "consecrate" instead of "sanctify." Jesus most certainly meant the last. (See the Appendix under "Sanctify" for a further discussion of the subject.)

It is of interest to know that the *Revised Standard Version* in its early editions also translated the verb here and elsewhere "consecrate." A group of scholars headed by J. A. Huffman voiced a protest. The editors gave this careful attention, then acknowledged their error, and made one of the very few changes adopted in later editions, so that the word now reads "sanctify." It is unfortunate that other translators did not learn from this.

When Jesus requested that His disciples be made holy or become sanctified, He had three aspects in mind—three aspects of a single experience, essentially simultaneous and equally important. We turn to the Book of Acts, which records the fulfillment of Christ's prayer.

a. They were all "filled with the Holy Spirit" (Acts 2:4). He had previously spoken to them of "the Spirit of truth, whom the world cannot receive, because it does not behold Him or know Him, but you know Him because He abides *with* you, and will be *in* you" (John 14:17). It was quite evident that, while the Holy Spirit was entirely unknown to the world, He was known by, and did dwell in, the believer. For Jesus had plainly said, "Unless one is born of water and the Spirit, he cannot enter into the kingdom of God" (John 3:5). And Paul later wrote (Rom. 8:9): "If anyone does not have the Spirit of Christ, he does not belong to Him." But to be "born of" the Spirit and to "have" or "possess" the Spirit is quite different from being *"filled with"* the Spirit, to being *"possessed by"* Him. It isn't that a man receives more of the Spirit—the Spirit cannot be divided. But the Spirit comes to possess more—yes, all—of the man. This is an important part of what Jesus prayed for when He said, "Sanctify them." He wanted them to be Spirit-filled men.

b. In addition, their hearts were cleansed. They received "the blessing of a clean heart." Now, happily, there is much emphasis today on being filled with the Spirit. But, unfortunately, heart cleansing is often forgotten, or relegated to a secondary place. It is actually equally as important. Peter, some years after the event, was present in the church conference in Jerusalem, as recorded in Acts 15. When there had been "much debate" regarding how the Gentiles were to be received into the fellowship of the Church, Peter finally arose to make his observations. Recalling how God had sent him to evangelize the Gentiles, he spoke about those who believed, who became converts. Verse 7 says:

> And after there had been much debate, Peter stood up and said to them, "Brethren, you know that in the early days God made a choice among you, that by my mouth the Gentiles should hear the word of the gospel *and believe* [become converted]. And God, *who knows the heart* [its wickedness, its defilement], bore witness to them, *giving them the Holy Spirit,* just as He also did to us; and He made no distinction between us and them, *cleansing their hearts by faith."*

Note clearly that Peter's memory of what had happened to the 120 on the Day of Pentecost, some 15 years before, was not primarily that of "a noise like a violent, rushing wind"; not of "tongues as of fire distributing themselves," resting on each of them; not of their beginning "to speak with other tongues, as the Spirit was giving them utterance," but rather that *their* hearts had been *cleansed by faith.* And *this same cleansing* came to the Gentile converts as they too received the filling of the Holy Spirit.

And how these men needed cleansing! They already belonged to God; their names were written in heaven. But Peter may well have remembered with shame the "sins of the spirit" from which they had need of being cleansed. From subsequent teaching it is apparent that these stemmed from inherited depravity, variously known as Adamic sin, original sin, the principle of sin.

This cleansing, for example, needed to be applied to the spirit of vindictiveness manifested when two of them had wanted to call down fire from heaven to consume villagers who opposed Christ. The spirit of jealousy and divisiveness surfaced when they were disputing about who would be the greatest in Jesus' kingdom when He established it. The spirit of pride and self-importance was revealed when none of them was willing to wash feet at the Last Supper, and Jesus did it himself. That spirit of self-seeking became apparent when they said in essence, "We have left all. . . . What's in it for us?" The spirit of fearfulness was revealed when, in Gethsemane, they all forsook Him and fled; and when, later, they were gathered together behind closed doors "for fear of the Jews." Of all these Peter was reminded. But he also knew that from them they had been cleansed on that Day of Pentecost by faith in Christ's atonement. It had not been by their works nor by their merit. It had been a work of faith! They received the blessing of a clean heart.

Surely it was something of this which filled the heart of the Methodist minister James Nicholson when he wrote:

Lord Jesus, for this I most humbly entreat;
I wait, blessed Lord, at Thy crucified feet.
By faith for my cleansing I see Thy blood flow;
Now wash me, and I shall be whiter than snow.

c. The other aspect of their sanctification as requested by Jesus was an anointing for service, a preparation for witness. A few days after this prayer He had declared, "But you shall receive power when the Holy Spirit has come upon you; and you shall be My witnesses both in Jerusalem, and in all Judea and Samaria, and even to the remotest part of the earth" (Acts 1:8). This promised unction for action undoubtedly reminded Jesus of *His own* anointing which He associated with His baptism (Luke 4:18-19): "THE SPIRIT OF THE LORD IS UPON ME, BECAUSE HE [the Holy Spirit] *anointed Me* TO PREACH THE GOSPEL TO THE POOR. HE HAS SENT ME TO PROCLAIM RELEASE TO THE CAPTIVES, AND RECOVERY OF SIGHT TO THE BLIND, TO SET FREE THOSE WHO ARE DOWNTRODDEN, TO PROCLAIM THE FAVORABLE YEAR OF THE LORD." It was to be the moment His men became prepared to announce the good news. And it happened on the Day of Pentecost. His prayer was answered. They were sanctified.

Now examine the *type of action* involved. It all happened in a moment of time—suddenly. "Suddenly . . . they were all filled with the Holy Spirit." There was no prolonged process of filling. Suddenly their hearts were cleansed. It did not require years or even months to cleanse them. It took only an instant. Suddenly they were anointed for service. In a moment of time they were given power, and went forth immediately to witness, as seen in the succeeding chapters of Acts.

And that was the very way Jesus had requested it. His prayer "Sanctify them" is in the imperative mood, aorist tense. This is the Greek tense of action as "the event of a single whole"; the tense of "a happening"; the tense that identifies action as "punctiliar" and can be represented as a point, a dot; the tense of "a simple occurrence." This aorist tense is the tense, as may be surmised, of conversion: "You must be born again" (John 3:7); "Believe in the Lord Jesus, and you shall be saved" (Acts 16:31); "Therefore if any man is in Christ, he is a new creature; the old things passed away; behold, new things have come" (2 Cor. 5:17); "Being justified by faith, we have peace with God" (Rom. 5:1). Conversion is *an event*. Likewise, the sanctification that Jesus speaks of here is, like getting saved, *an event* of eternal importance.

This fact is overlooked by many theologians, who insist that sanctification is not a crisis, only a process. In this they are only half right.

Bishop Moule has aptly expressed it: "Sanctification is a crisis with a view to a process; or a process beginning with a crisis."

That is how Jesus defined it!

Sanctification is not only "an event of a single whole"; it is *also* a growth, a subsequent process of progress in holy living. This fact is inherent in the Greek. For the tense changes from the restricted aorist tense of *an event* ("Sanctify them") to the *continuing present* tense of *progressive* sanctification ("that they themselves also may *be* [continually, progressively] sanctified" or in a sanctified experience). Wuest declares: "When a Greek uses the present tense rather than the aorist tense he is going out of his way to emphasize *durative* action."[1] Thus Jesus went out of His way to show that sanctification as He provided for it in the atonement is *first a crisis* (v. 17), *then a process* (v. 19).

Thus holiness is not static. It is an experience in which to grow, in which to have new or repeated sacred experiences, in which to become more and more like Jesus in mature Christian character.

This progressive sanctification will include frequent and, indeed, continuous cleansings (1 John 1:7): "The blood of Jesus His Son [continually, present tense] cleanses us from all sin." For, although basically cleansed of inherited depravity at the time of entire sanctification, the Christian is constantly exposed to the sordid influence of the world. From this he needs constant cleansing. Even as the eye, although quite pure of itself, requires frequent cleansings from the impurities of the air, so the soul needs a continual washing.

This progressive sanctification will include frequent infillings of the Spirit. Eph. 5:18 exhorts, "Be filled with the Spirit." The word "filled" is in the present, durative tense of continuous or repeated action. "Be repeatedly or continuously filled," or "be being filled." Thus Acts 4:31 records that the disciples, only a few weeks after Pentecost, again "were all filled with the Holy Spirit."

This continuing sanctification makes possible uninterrupted, victorious living, for "in all these things we overwhelmingly conquer [again and again, present tense] through Him who loved us" (Rom. 8:37). It will include constant growth (2 Pet. 3:18): "But grow in the grace and knowledge of our Lord and Savior Jesus Christ." Here "grow" is in the present tense of persistence.

Note now our Lord's statement in v. 19: "I sanctify [consecrate] Myself, that they themselves may be sanctified." As Paul expressed it (Eph. 5:25), "Christ also loved the church and gave Himself up for her; that He might sanctify her." *Christ's love and His atoning act were not just for the need of godless people of the world, that they might become saved* (John 3:16); *but also for the need of His own people, that they might become sanctified.* This is an awesome, all-important fact of Calvary. Paul recognized that twofold purpose of the Cross when he wrote Titus (2:14), "Who gave Himself for us, that HE MIGHT REDEEM US FROM EVERY LAWLESS DEED AND PURIFY FOR HIMSELF A PEOPLE FOR HIS OWN POSSESSION, zealous for good deeds." Note "redeem" *and* "purify."

Furthermore, the experience of sanctification is not for the cloistered life, nor is it essentially for personal enjoyment—not even just that we may have a victorious life. Its purpose is that the man of God may be prepared to be sent "into the world," even as our Lord was sent by His Father into the world (v. 18). The one who would properly represent his Lord must penetrate a dying world with a living gospel.

Nor can we forget that He said: "I do not ask in behalf of these alone, but *for those also who believe in Me through their word."* We are part of that "apostolic succession."

5. There is a final aspect to our Lord's prayer, namely, that they *be kept as a "glorious" church.* "That they may behold My glory, which Thou hast given Me" (v. 24); for "the glory which Thou hast given Me I have given to them" (v. 22). Paul caught the spirit of this when he wrote, "But we all, with unveiled face beholding as in a mirror

the glory of the Lord, are being transformed into the same image *from glory to glory,* just as from the Lord, the Spirit" (2 Cor. 3:18). And again, after saying that Christ desired to sanctify His Church, Paul continued (Eph. 5: 27): "That He might present to Himself the church *in all her glory,* having no spot or wrinkle or any such thing; but that she should [continually, present tense] be holy and blameless."

And the world rightfully looks for that glory in God's children.

Those present in Cleveland at one of the annual conventions of the National Holiness Association will long remember the witness of Dr. John L. Brasher to that great convention. Because of age and infirmity he was unable to be present in person, but was invited to give his testimony over the long-distance telephone. The message was relayed to the convention via the loudspeakers in the large auditorium.

Having made the connections, the president of the association invited Dr. Brasher to relate how he had come into the blessing of holiness. "Gladly," he responded. His voice came clear and loud. "It was not long after the turn of the century and I, an eager theological student, went to hear one Samuel Logan Brengle, armed with all the arguments against the doctrine I knew he would preach."

The convention crowd gave close attention to every word as it came over the telephone. "But even as I listened," continued Dr. Brasher, "marshaling all my arguments, I lost track of what he actually was saying, and became captivated by his face, his voice, his mannerisms. I had found the answer to my arguments, not in his logic, which probably was entirely sound, but in his very attitude, in his projection of God's glory. That night I found the blessing. That night I commenced a life of holiness that has been sufficient for more than half a century."

And he ended his witness with that expression so characteristic of Commissioner Brengle himself, "Hallelujah!"

Turn your eyes upon Jesus,
  Look full in His wonderful face,
And the things of earth will grow strangely dim
  In the light of His glory and grace.

In summary, Jesus established that the sanctification He would offer through His sacrifice was to be an experience reserved for, needed by, and attainable by *every* child of God. It was to be a crisis experience of cleansing, of filling, of anointing subsequent to salvation, and then an experience of continued progress and victory and growth. It was to be an experience essential to being sent "into the world" with the gospel. It would be an experience, not just for the disciples of His day, but for all believers of every age and generation. And, finally, it would bring a "glow of glory" into the lives of all its recipients.

PART II:
What Paul Said

6

*What Paul said
to the church in Thessalonica about being*

Wholly Sanctified

1 THESSALONIANS

From the viewpoint of its teaching on holiness, the First Epistle to the Thessalonians is intriguing—and vastly important. It contains Paul's first recorded statements on the doctrine. In addition, it is accepted by many as the first Christian literature to be preserved as part of Holy Writ. (See "Chronology of the New Testament" in the Appendix.)

What Paul may have known of Christ's message we can only surmise, for he was not present during our Lord's ministries. We must suppose, however, that, although the Gospels had not yet been committed to writing, the contents of our Lord's various teachings on holy living, and then His impassioned plea later recorded in John 17, were often discussed and freely disseminated by the 11 men who were present. Furthermore, this letter, 1 Thessalonians, must surely reflect a knowledge on Paul's part of the happenings on the Day of Pentecost and of the marked change made in the disciples at that time. He would be aware of the effect on the converts mentioned by Peter in Acts 15—how, upon receipt of the Holy Spirit, their hearts likewise were cleansed by faith. He would certainly have his own testimony of sanctification upon which to rely.

Thessalonica was a young church. In a brief visit, possibly of only three weeks (Acts 17:1-10), conviction of sin had descended on many who were raw heathens and they had turned from their false idols to the true and living God (1 Thess. 1:9). In spite of "much tribulation" (1:6) and "sufferings at the hands of your own countrymen" (2:14; 3:3-4), they had, in Paul's evaluation, become "imitators of us and of the Lord" and "an example to all the believers in Macedonia and in Achaia" (1:6-7). Of that Paul was justly proud (2:19-20). By their faith he was comforted (3:7). In them he openly rejoiced (3:9).

Yet there was something lacking in their faith (3:10); something so important that, after being separated from them but a short time (2:17, literally "a few hours"), Paul now writes urgently to this young church regarding their hearts becoming established in holiness (3:13). He then outlines the moral aspect of holiness (4:1-7; 5:12-22); and, finally, the comprehensive nature of entire sanctification (5:23).

Now it must not be supposed that this was the only reason for the letter. This young church was excited about the return of Christ. Some of the believers were worrying about those who had died or who might die before His return (4:13). Some were neglecting the practical matter of earning a livelihood in their earnest expectation of the *parousia*—the coming of their Lord (4:11-12; 2 Thess. 3:10-12). Others were particularly exercised about the appearing of "the son of destruction" (2 Thess. 2:3f.). To these honest questioners Paul expounded some of the most exquisite and explicit answers to be found in the Bible on the second coming of our Lord. These letters to the Thessalonians are known for their precise teachings regarding "last things." In that respect alone they are priceless.

For our present study, however, it is interesting to

observe that, in the light of the anticipated coming of our Lord, it was incumbent upon the Church that it be holy, pure, sanctified. He will come "to be glorified in His saints on that day" (2 Thess. 1:10). *For this they must be prepared now, while in the midst of life, and not then, in the midst of climactic crisis.*

There are essentially two aspects to this teaching as expounded here by Paul—the part God will do, and the part man must do. Let us note the latter first.

1. There is the frank, candid, and *encouraging* exhortation regarding man's responsibilities and the ethics of holy living.

> Finally then, brethren, we request and exhort you in the Lord Jesus that, as you received from us instruction as to how you ought to walk and please God *(just as you actually do walk),* that you may excel *still more.* For you know what commandments we gave you by the authority of the Lord Jesus. For this is the will of God, your sanctification; that is, that you abstain from sexual immorality [Greek, "*continue* to abstain"; they already were abstaining] *(4:1-3).*

Then, after outlining some of the details of the passions common to the Gentiles and previously practiced by them, he continues: "For God has not called us for the purpose of impurity, but in sanctification. Consequently, he who rejects this is not rejecting man but the God who gives His Holy Spirit to you" (4:7-8).

A further sample of what man must do if he is to exhibit holy living is outlined in Christian duties similar in spirit to Christ's Beatitudes, recorded by Paul in the fifth chapter. And again he encourages them, in that they were already doing many of these things.

> Therefore, encourage one another, and build up one another, *just as you also are doing.* But we request of you, brethren, that you appreciate those who diligently labor among you, and have charge over you in the Lord

and give you instruction, and that you esteem them very highly in love because of their work. Live in peace with one another. And we urge you, brethren, admonish the unruly, encourage the fainthearted, help the weak, be patient with all men. See that no one repays another with evil for evil, but always seek after that which is good for one another and for all men. Rejoice always; pray without ceasing; in everything give thanks; for this is God's will for you in Christ Jesus. Do not quench the Spirit; do not despise prophetic utterances. But examine everything carefully; hold fast to that which is good; abstain from every form of evil *(5:11-22).*

Paul was being very straightforward—and fundamental—with this infant church in the matter of practical sanctification. Holiness was to be a life, not a theory. It must reflect man's will and spiritual hunger as well as God's longing and provision.

Let it here be noted that much of that which may be known as victorious living, as leading a holy and godly life, is related to man's continued efforts, his restatements of purpose, his renewed consecrations.

In this our hymn writers are of great help to us.

> *Stand up, stand up for Jesus,*
> *Ye soldiers of the Cross.*
> *Lift high His royal banner;*
> *It must not suffer loss.*
> *From vict'ry unto vict'ry*
> *His army shall He lead,*
> *Till ev'ry foe is vanquished,*
> *And Christ is Lord indeed.*

* * *

> *A charge to keep I have,*
> *A God to glorify;*
> *A never-dying soul to save,*
> *And fit it for the sky.*

* * *

*O Master, let me walk with Thee
In lowly paths of service free.
Tell me Thy secret; help me bear
The strain of toil, the fret of care.*

* * *

*Take my life, and let it be
Consecrated, Lord, to Thee.
Take my moments and my days;
Let them flow in ceaseless praise.*

Indeed, man's responsibility to holy living is as old as God's Word. Through Moses, God had commanded: "For I am the Lord your God: ye shall therefore sanctify yourselves, and ye shall be holy; for I am holy" (Lev. 11:44, KJV).

In all this, of course, Paul was also complying with the teaching and standards set by Jesus. In outlining what *God* would do in our sanctification Paul also complied with the teaching of his Lord.

2. The doctrinal passages in this Epistle regarding *God's* part in man's sanctification are two—two prayers which conclude chapters 3 and 5 respectively.

Note the urgency.

We night and day keep praying most earnestly that we may see your face, and may complete *what is lacking in your faith.* Now may our God and Father Himself and Jesus our Lord direct our way to you; and may the Lord cause you to increase and abound in love for one another, and for all men, just as we also do for you; so *that He may establish your hearts unblamable in holiness before our God and Father* at the coming of our Lord Jesus with all His saints *(3:10-13).*

And again:

Now may the God of peace Himself *sanctify you entirely;* and may your spirit and soul and body be preserved complete, *without blame* at the coming of our Lord Jesus Christ *(5:23).*

Whatever man may and must do toward living a holy life, it is God, and God only, who can establish hearts in holiness, who can sanctify entirely.

a. Concentrating now on these passages by Paul, let us make comparison with our Lord's teaching as recorded in John 17. In the eyes of both there is an importance—yes, an urgency—for the Christian to become sanctified. Jesus made it the heart of His great final prayer: "Sanctify them." Paul recognized it as *that which was lacking* in the faith of his people. This importance cannot be denied and must not be treated lightly.

General Frederick L. Coutts has said:

> The doctrine of holiness should always be considered in its proper setting—as an integral part of the redemptive purpose of God for men. Rightly understood it is the one serious attempt which believers may make (as God shall help them) to translate the spirit of Jesus into a recognizable pattern of Christian behaviour. The forgiven soul cannot be content to remain forgiven only. ... When theologians declare that "a justification which does not issue in sanctification is not justification at all," they are but saying in their own idiom what simpler believers instinctively realize.[1]

b. With both Paul and Jesus, *it is God's work.* Jesus called out, "Father, *You* must sanctify these My disciples." Paul prayed to the end "that *He* [God] may establish" their hearts in holiness, and again that "the God of peace *Himself* [might] sanctify" them entirely.

c. Jesus saw it as an experience not only for His immediate family of 11 men, but more particularly for His *great* family of all believers. Paul now dared apply this to his little group of redeemed idol worshippers—people who had never known God through His old covenant with Israel nor had any religious advantage whatsoever. Furthermore, a long Christian apprenticeship was not required. The Thessalonians had been saved only a few months, perhaps only a few weeks. They needed to be sanctified, and that, now.

d. Furthermore, as with the disciples, this was to be with the Thessalonians a work of grace *subsequent* to their conversion. As has been noted, Paul was justly proud of his spiritual church which set such a good example to other churches. They were already "well saved."

e. Again, as it was in our Lord's petition, so it was with Paul's prayer, that this was to be an *event* of importance in their lives. For, as did our Lord, so did Paul—he used the aorist tense, the tense of action as of a single whole: "that He may *stablish* [in a moment of time] your hearts unblamable in holiness"; "Now may the God of peace Himself *sanctify* you entirely [as a crisis experience]," in as clean a break as when "you *turned* to God from idols to serve a living and true God" (1:9). In each case the italicized word is in the aorist tense, denoting a completed act. Paul believed God would do it again as at Pentecost—"suddenly"!

Dr. Adam Clarke has expressed it that we are to come to God for as instantaneous and complete a purification from all sin as for an instantaneous pardon. "In no part of the Scripture are we directed to seek the remission of our sins *seriatim*—one now and another then, and so on." He continues,

> Neither a gradation pardon nor a gradation purification exists in the Bible. For, as the work of renewing and cleansing the heart is the work of God, His almighty power can perform it in a moment, in the twinkling of an eye. And it is *this moment* our duty to love God with all our heart, and we cannot do this until He cleanses our hearts. Consequently *He is ready to do it this moment.* Believing now, we are pardoned now; believing now, we are cleansed from all sin now.

f. Paul also prayed for a *continuing* experience among his people—that their hearts might not only be *established* in holiness, but also that their spirits and souls and bodies be *preserved* without blame unto the coming of our Lord Jesus Christ. He apparently remembered that Jesus had prayed that His disciples might (continually) be sanctified in truth.

g. As Jesus had expressed His deep *desire* that His men be sanctified, so Paul declared, "For this is the *will of God,* your sanctification."

In further comments, Frederick Coutts declared:

> Paul, writing his first letter calling his converts to Christian holiness, said: "For ye know what commandments we gave you by the Lord Jesus. For this is the will of God, even your sanctification." Note, first of all, that the Apostle was not saying to his converts: "You can be holy because you long to be holy"—though doubtless this was their desire as it is ours. Nor did he say: "You can be holy for I long to see you enter into this experience"—though that must have been one of his dearest wishes. His counsel was this: *God's will* is that you be holy. This grace was founded neither on human wishes nor on the hopes of a leader, but on the express will of God.[2]

h. The *need* and the *reason* for this experience are not hard to find. The Salvation Army's fifth point of doctrine states precisely the position held by all holiness bodies, namely, that "in consequence of their fall, all men have become sinners, totally depraved." However, these words do not imply that, as sinners, men are either completely evil or are incapable of greater wickedness. Rather, the depravity of the sinner is total in the sense that *every part of the being is affected* by the corruption of sin. As Wiley says: "The term is not used *intensively,* but rather *extensively.* It is a contagion spread through man's entire being. With this, man is born. Theologians call it 'original sin,' 'Adamic sin,' 'inbred sin.'"[3] Paul, in his letter to the Romans, simply calls it "the sin." It is "the hereditary tendency of men toward evil."

It is specifically to deal with this *inherited* depravity that Paul petitions his God. Now there is an *acquired* depravity, which is dealt with at conversion in what is sometimes called "*initial* sanctification." With the Thessalonians a multitude of wicked practices are summed up under their having "served idols." When they got saved they turned from these practices. So every sinner is expected to put away, at conversion, his outward sins which characterize his acquired depravity—lying, stealing, immorality, drunkenness. But generally *he is unaware of his inherited depravity.* It is later that he becomes aware of it in an inner unrest, a bitter conflict as described by Paul in Romans 7 (which will be examined in detail later). But God will not deny the hunger of the heart. He has provided an *entire* sanctification to deal with the inherited corruption. Paul is here describing this.

i. Then, in positive ways, Paul, through divine inspiration, enlarges and more specifically *defines* the event known as entire sanctification. "Now may the God of peace Himself sanctify you entirely [or wholly, or through and through]; and may your spirit and soul and body be preserved complete [or entire or whole], without blame at [or until] the coming of our Lord Jesus Christ."

Ralph Earle says of this: "The emphasis here is on the sanctifying of the entire human personality, resulting in its integration and preservation. This 'through and through' sanctification meets the requirements of modern psychology as no other experience does."[4] W. O. Klopfenstein observes that

> the thoroughness of sanctification is clearly indicated. The sanctifying act is designed to penetrate and permeate not only the conscious nature of the believer but

also the subconscious strata of his personality. Salvation is not only all of grace; salvation not only provides grace for all who choose to accept it; but this salvation also provides grace for the *whole* man, as Paul indeed prays.[5]

j. This act of sanctification is called *"entire"* in the light of the descriptive words "wholly" and "whole." For it acts "wholly" upon the "whole" or complete man, in the very areas affected by the Fall. It will affect "wholly" his "whole spirit"—that is, his attitude, his mood, his demeanor (1 Tim. 4:12). It will affect "wholly" his "whole soul"—the seat of the will (Luke 1:46), of the affections (Matt. 26:38), of the reasoning (Acts 14:2; Phil. 1:27). It will affect "wholly" his "whole body"—the physical, temporal part of man, which is to be presented to God "holy" (Rom. 12:1) and which is the home of the Holy Spirit (1 Cor. 6:19). Thus this experience of entire sanctification leaves no part of the personality untouched. It affects all the faculties through which man has relationship with God, with himself, with other men.

> *Through and through, through and through,*
>   *Jesus, make me holy;*
> *Save me to the uttermost*
>   *All the way to glory.*

k. Paul introduces a most meaningful word, first in personal testimony (2:10) and then in promise (3:13; 5:23). The word is *amemptos,* variously translated "unblamable," "without blame," "blameless," "above reproach"—but *not* "faultless." It is a perfection of *purpose,* of *intent.* It is not a perfection of *performance,* which will be possible only in heaven. Mistakes there may be, but sins there need not be.

The recognition of this is one of the important contributions of John Wesley to theology—that blameworthy sins are of the will, the mind, the purpose. For them man is responsible. From them he may be delivered. For sins of ignorance, of misunderstanding, men are not responsible. Thus man may be blameless, but not faultless. The important words are *intent, purpose.* My child or grandchild, too young to understand, helps out by "weeding" the garden. But the "weeds" removed often include the carefully nurtured flowers. He certainly is not *faultless,* but, bless his heart, he may be *blameless.* The purpose and intent of his heart are above blame. And thus, indeed, had Jesus defined Christian perfection (Matt. 5:48).

We thank Paul for introducing that word *amemptos* to the Scriptures.

Did Paul add verse 24 from personal experience? "Faithful is He who calls you [to holiness], and He also will bring it to pass." At any rate we thank God because it is true!

> *Here I stand, myself disdaining,*
>   *While the Spirit passes by;*
> *Stand in faith, Thy mercy claiming,*
>   *While the Spirit passes by.*
> *Let Thy power my soul refine,*
> *Let Thy grace my will incline,*
> *Take my all and make it Thine,*
>   *While the Spirit passes by.*
>   —HERBERT H. BOOTH

*What Paul said
to "the church . . . at Corinth" concerning*

God's Pattern for Perfection

2 COR. 7:1

If we are to give any recognition to an increasing maturity of spiritual understanding on the part of Paul and a "progressive revelation" from God to him, it will be significant to note that this Corinthian letter was written four or five years after his letter to the Thessalonians. (See "Chronology of the New Testament" in the Appendix.)

It is true that Paul was writing to an entirely different type of church, and for quite different reasons. It would seem, then, that he is presenting the *same doctrine* of sanctification, but with a different emphasis and in differing details.

> Therefore, having these promises, beloved, let us cleanse ourselves from all defilement of flesh and spirit, perfecting holiness in the fear of God *(2 Cor. 7:1)*.

The Corinthian church was not a young church, as was the one at Thessalonica. Paul had ministered there more than a year and a half (Acts 18:11, 18), building upon the faithful work of a godly couple, Aquila and Priscilla. It was also a Gentile church (v. 6), but the people were not really neophytes after this comparatively long nurturing, by the Apostle Paul, "teaching the word of God among them."

They *were* saved (1 Cor. 1:18-21, 30-31; 3:5). Indeed they were "sanctified" (1:2; 6:9-11). But this was an *initial* sanctification, a cleansing of *acquired* depravity. Paul enumerates an awesome list of sins from which they were cleansed at the time of their conversion:

> Do not be deceived; neither fornicators, nor idolaters, nor adulterers, nor effeminate, nor homosexuals, nor thieves, nor covetous, nor drunkards, nor revilers, nor swindlers, shall inherit the kingdom of God. And such were some of you; but you were *washed,* but you were *sanctified,* but you were *justified* in the name of the Lord Jesus Christ, and in the Spirit of our God *(1 Cor. 6:9-11).*

Now this is true conversion. They were not only forgiven or justified of these coarse sins; they were also *delivered* from them—"washed, sanctified, justified." *Nothing less than this can be called true conversion.*

But, as we shall see, they were still carnal—a jealous, contentious people, divided, argumentative, irreverent. In his first letter to them, apparently written four or five years after being with them, Paul was forced to deal harshly and unsparingly with them regarding these faults.

Now a few more months had passed. Paul had gone on from Ephesus to Macedonia, probably in A.D. 56. But, constrained by what he felt to be criticism of him and his ministry, he wrote a very personal and, in some ways, defensive letter answering their criticism. This Epistle reveals the humanity of the great apostle more than any other of his writings.

It does not lend itself too well to an outline. However, chapters 3 through 6 speak to the various facets of Paul's ministry, and are thus worth noting.

1. Certified by his converts (3:1-3)
2. Centered in the new covenant (3:4-6)
3. Characterized by glory (3:7—4:6)
4. Circumscribed by human limitations (4:7—5:8)

    5. Compelled by deep convictions (5:9-21)
    6. Commended by testings (6:1-13)
    7. Climaxed by a plea for holiness (6:14—7:1)

Observe that the last is a fitting climax to his ministry for these people. This church needed holiness.

The text (7:1) naturally divides itself into three parts, featuring the three verbs *"having," cleansing,* and *"perfecting."*

1. "Having" or possessing "these promises" is a prerequisite to all that follows.

a. Note first the *substance* of the promises as listed in 6:16-18. *"I will dwell in them"*—possession; *"walk among them"*—fellowship; *"be their God, and they . . . My people"*—protection; and, above all, *"be a father to you, and you shall be sons and daughters to Me"*—adoption.

These promises do not apply to humanity in general, however. One must beware of the "universal fatherhood of God" idea. In a *generic* sense He is the Father of all. There is "one God and Father of all" (Eph. 4:6). "For in Him we live and move and exist, even as one of your own poets have said, 'For we also are His offspring'" (Acts 17:28). But *spiritually, no.* Paul clearly declared: "Among them we too all formerly lived in the lusts of our flesh . . . and were by nature children of wrath, even as the rest" (Eph. 2:3). And, of course, Jesus boldly proclaimed to the rebellious unbelievers of His day, "You are of your father the devil" (John 8:44).

b. As Christians, we may rejoice in the *privileges* of having or possessing these promises. "But as many as received Him, to them gave He the right to become children of God, even to those who believe in His name" (John 1:12). Again, "But when the fulness of the time came, God sent forth His Son, born of a woman, born under the Law, in order that He might redeem those who were under the

Law, that we might receive the adoption as sons" (Gal. 4:4-5). And again, "For you have not received a spirit of slavery leading to fear again, but you have received a spirit of adoption as sons by which we cry out, 'Abba! Father!'" (Rom. 8:15).

For there *are* distinct privileges in being the children of God.

The servant in the king's household serves quietly, respectfully, coming and going as he is bidden, occupying his place in the servants' quarters. But the son, the heir, comes in by the front door; enters the very presence of the king unbidden; enjoys the fellowship, the protection, and the possessions of being the son of the king.

We who know the privilege of being children of God can, with the poet, Hattie Buell, sing:

"My Father is rich in houses and lands;
He holdeth the wealth of the world in His hands.
Of rubies and diamonds, of silver and gold,
His coffers are full; He has riches untold.
   [For]
I'm the child of a King;
The child of a King;
   With Jesus, my Saviour,
I'm the child of a King!"

c. But there is a *condition* to possessing these promises. The condition is *separation*. Paul warned the Corinthians:

Do not be bound together with unbelievers; for what partnership have righteousness and lawlessness, or what fellowship has light with darkness? Or what harmony has Christ with Belial, or what has a believer in common with an unbeliever? Or what agreement has the temple of God with idols? For we are the temple of the living God. . . . "Therefore, COME OUT FROM THEIR MIDST AND BE SEPARATE, says the Lord, AND DO NOT TOUCH WHAT IS UNCLEAN; AND I WILL WELCOME YOU. AND I WILL

BE A FATHER TO YOU, AND YOU SHALL BE SONS and daughters TO ME, SAYS THE LORD ALMIGHTY" *(2 Cor. 6:14-18).*

In a realistic fashion this is an enlargement of our Lord's prayer, "Keep them from the evil" (John 17:15). It was a call, not that they should be taken out of the world, but that they should be kept from worldliness, from "partnership" with "lawlessness," from "fellowship" with "darkness." This is the cost of sonship.

d. There are, likewise, the *responsibilities* of possessing these promises. The child of a king must act like one. There is a dignity, a royal demeanor, a distinctiveness he must maintain.

A story is told that at the time of the French Revolution the revolutionaries, after slaying the king and most of the royalty, took into custody one of the young princes. "We will degrade him," they boasted. "We will break his spirit and debase his manners and morals until he is no better than a serf, a common slave." Accordingly they subjected him to all indignities, put him under the demeaning influence of foul-mouthed, uncouth tutors. Perplexed, then bewildered, he faced these unaccustomed circumstances for a term. Finally, he rebelled. Facing his tormentors with courage, he drew his little self up to his full height and declared boldly: "This I will not do; these things I will not say; thus I will not live. *I was born to be a king!"*

In the context of our text it is obvious that Paul was declaring that they who "had," who "possessed" these promises qualified as "children of God," as born-again believers. It was they who should—indeed, *only* they who could—benefit by cleansing.

Paul is setting the standards of being God's sons and daughters on a high level. Don't sell short the privilege of being a child of God.

2. It is to them that Paul presents his challenge—the second verb in our text—*cleansing.*

a. In line with the prayer of our Lord for His disciples and the previously recorded petition by Paul for the Thessalonians, it should not be surprising to learn that the admonition "Let us cleanse ourselves" is in the aorist tense; the tense of a single, outstanding event. The cleansing is to be a *positive act* at a point of time. H. Orton Wiley has declared: "Purity is the result of a cleansing from the pollution of sin; maturity is due to growth in grace. Purity is accomplished by an instantaneous act; maturity is gradual and progressive, and is always indefinite and relative."[1]

b. Such a cleansing for God's people is entirely *scriptural.* Through Isaiah the Israelites were commanded: "Wash yourselves, make yourselves clean; remove the evil of your deeds from My sight. Cease to do evil, learn to do good" (1:16-17). It is promised through Ezekiel: "Then I will sprinkle clean water on you, and you will be clean; I will cleanse you from all your filthiness and from all your idols" (36:25).

Such a cleansing is divinely provided: "Christ also loved the church and gave Himself up for her; that He might sanctify her, having cleansed her by the washing of water with the word" (Eph. 5:25-26). It is divinely rewarded: "Blessed are the pure in heart, for they shall see God" (Matt. 5:8). Thus, it is indeed the privilege of all believers to be wholly sanctified.

The longing is expressed by Samuel Hodges in the verses:

> *Tell me what to do to be pure*
> *In the sight of the all-seeing Eyes;*
> *Tell me, is there no thorough cure,*
> *No escape from the sin I despise?*

> *Tell me, can I never be free*
> *From this terrible bondage within?*
> *Is there no deliverance for me*
> *From the thraldom of indwelling sin?*

He then answers his own question in the chorus:

> *Whiter than the snow!*
> *Wash me in the blood of the Lamb,*
> *And I shall be whiter than snow.*

c. This cleansing of the believer also is completely *practical*. The verse speaks of "defilement." The Greek word is *molusmos* and is used only here in the New Testament. It is variously translated as "defilement," "filthiness," "contamination." It reminds me of a contaminated well we had for our water supply from which my brother got typhoid fever. The well had to be "cleansed" thoroughly. The verse says "all"—which is the same word used by John when he spoke of "all sin" and "all unrighteousness" (1 John 1:7, 9).

It was in his first letter to them that Paul had described to the Corinthians something of their "defilement" which marked them as "men of flesh," "fleshly," or, as in the KJV, "carnal." The Greek for this adjective is a derivative of *sarx*, which Paul will refer to in his second letter.

But read now from his first letter the listing of their shortcomings.

> Now I exhort you, brethren, by the name of our Lord Jesus Christ, that you all agree, and there be no divisions among you, but you be made complete in the same mind and in the same judgment. For I have been informed concerning you, my brethren, by Chloe's people, that there are quarrels among you *(1 Cor. 1:10-11)*.

> A natural man does not accept the things of the Spirit of God; for they are foolishness to him, and he cannot understand them, because they are spiritually

appraised. But he who is spiritual appraises all things, yet he himself is appraised by no man. For WHO HAS KNOWN THE MIND OF THE LORD, THAT HE SHOULD INSTRUCT HIM? But we have the mind of Christ *(1 Cor. 2:14-16)*.

And I, brethren, could not speak to you as to spiritual men, but as to men of flesh, as to babes in Christ. I gave you milk to drink, not solid food; for you were not yet able to receive it. Indeed, even now you are not yet able, for you are still fleshly. For since there is jealousy and strife among you, are you not fleshly, and are you not walking like mere men? For when one says, "I am of Paul," and another, "I am of Apollos," are you not mere men? *(1 Cor. 3:1-4)*.

Paul here defined three types of men. The "natural man" is without Christ—unsaved. The "spiritual" man is spiritually minded—a Spirit-filled Christian. Then there is the man of the "flesh"—the "carnal" Christian. The Corinthians belonged to this third class. They were divisive, quarrelsome, jealous, contentious. They persisted in being "babes in Christ" who would not grow up. They were not childlike, but childish, persisting in their petty selfishness.

In his second letter, Paul is exhorting the Corinthian church to be rid of all this: "Let us cleanse ourselves from all defilement of flesh and spirit." Here is the noun *sarx*, now translated "flesh." While this word commonly refers to "the soft substance of the human body" (1 Cor. 15:39; 2 Cor. 12:7; et al.), it also may refer to man's depraved nature (Gal. 5:19-21, 24, et al.). Either of these could apply here. However, in the light of the nature of their sins of the spirit, the latter seems much more appropriate.

In a very unscientific manner we suggest leaving the *h* off "flesh" and spelling it backwards, which identifies it truly as *self*. (Actually, that is what Jesus calls the ingrained, wrong spirit of a man—"self"—which must be denied.) The adjective of course would then be *selfish*.

These Corinthian believers, though saved from many gross and fearsome sins, were still self-centered, selfish. From this they needed cleansing. From this do not all Christians need cleansing? For too often the sins of the spirit prevail.

d. Again, the cleansing is *effectual.* According to Acts 15:8 it is the same God "who knows the heart"—its filthiness and contamination, its selfishness and bent toward sinning—who applies a cleansing to those who come to Him by faith.

3. Which brings us to the third verb in Paul's text, "perfecting," or more fully, "perfecting holiness." (It should be noted that, as in John 17:17, so here there are translations which render *hagiadzo* as "consecrate." See Appendix under "Sanctify" for further comment on this.)

a. Observe first the *nature* of this action. It is continuing, persistent, and follows the triumph of cleansing. Regarding this, Julian C. McPheeters has said: "The verb perfecting is used here in the present tense indicating that the process is continuous. . . . Indeed, both a crisis and a continuous process are involved in the perfecting of holiness, and in this chapter we have emphasis upon both the crisis and the process of holiness."[2]

Nor is this inconsistent with our Lord's prayer that His disciples might *suddenly* be sanctified, and then *continually* be sanctified (John 17:17, 19); nor with Paul's prayer that the God of peace thoroughly sanctify the Thessalonians as a crisis act, and then that their sanctification be preserved (1 Thess. 5:23).

Daniel Steele wrote regarding "perfecting holiness":

> Here is the scope for progressive sanctification, through a prayerful culture of our intellects, attaining more light today in which to see yesterday's mistakes, and avoiding them in the future. Hence the duty enjoined in II Cor. 7:1, of perfecting holiness, is a progres-

sive work, realizing or carrying into practice, that cleansing from all filthiness (which has been) instantaneously wrought within.[3]

b. Note now the *verb itself,* "perfecting" *(epitileo).* According to the Greek lexicon it has a twofold meaning: first, to execute or carry into practice or perform regularly; and second, to mature, to bring to full stature, to ripen.

And that's the way with progressive sanctification. First of all, you put it to work. It must operate in every facet of life—the workshop, the school, the social life, business. *It belongs in all these places.* Secondly, it will mature; it will come to a full stature; it will "ripen" into the full fruit of the Spirit.

In the impressionable years of my youth we lived on a fruit farm in Colorado. In the early spring the peaches were "cleansed from all filthiness" by a spraying job. Then water came in irrigation ditches, and the sun shone. And the peaches, day by day, were "perfected." It took time to grow a luscious Mountain Lion brand peach. But, believe me, it was worth it.

Paul expressed it elsewhere: "Until we all attain to the unity of the faith, and of the knowledge of the Son of God, to a mature man, to the measure of the stature which belongs to the fulness of Christ" (Eph. 4:13).

8

*What Paul said
to the "beloved of God in Rome" about*

Sin in the Believer

ROMANS 6—8

It was during his third missionary tour, about a year after he had written to the Corinthians, that Paul also wrote his massive doctrinal Epistle to the Romans from Corinth. Impressively profound, it may well be the letter Peter referred to when he said: "Just as also our beloved brother Paul, according to the wisdom given him, wrote to you, as also in all his letters, speaking in them of these things, in which are *some things hard to understand*" (2 Pet. 3:15-16). If some things Paul wrote were hard for *Peter* to understand, we can be forgiven if we too find them deep and sometimes perplexing. But the Book of Romans is basic if we are to comprehend God's attitude toward mankind in its sinful condition. God had given Paul penetrating insight. Romans is possibly the peak of his writings.

Let us do some considered speculation. As previously proposed, Paul could hardly be ignorant of our Lord's great high-priestly prayer of some 30 years before. On the very eve of His crucifixion, Jesus, out of a heart of anguish and concern, had prayed that His disciples, above all, might be sanctified. He would also be aware of the impressive and historic answer to that prayer on the Day of Pentecost. He could hardly be ignorant of the dynamic power in the years that followed, of the Spirit-filled Church as recorded in the Book of Acts.

And he certainly was a party to the transformation of the lives of Gentiles upon receipt of the Holy Spirit as reported by Peter at the great church conference in Jerusalem convened some seven or eight years previously, as recorded in Acts 15. For Paul was there. And Peter was reporting both for himself and for Paul when he said, "And God, who knows the heart, bore witness to them, giving them the Holy Spirit, just as He also did to us; and He made no distinction between us and them, cleansing their hearts by faith."

These historic facts would be vivid in his mind as Paul meditated in Corinth. Then, moved by the Holy Spirit, he took up his pen to write to the church in Rome.

Since he had not yet been in Rome himself, the letter did not bear the personal observations or admonitions other letters did. But he would be in immediate memory of the guileless, earnest church in Thessalonica to whom, some four or five years previously, he had written, "We night and day keep praying most earnestly that we may see your face, and may complete what is lacking in your faith . . . that He may establish your hearts unblamable in holiness before our God and Father" (1 Thess. 3:10-13).

He would have vivid memories of his cantankerous church at Corinth, to whom, a few months before, he had written the urgent exhortation "Therefore, having these promises, beloved, let us cleanse ourselves from all defilement of flesh and spirit, perfecting holiness in the fear of God" (2 Cor. 7:1).

He would be immediately conscious of the vacillating Christians in the churches of Galatia, to whom he also wrote at this time. They were "so quickly deserting Him who called you by the grace of Christ, for a different gospel" (1:6). To them he gave his stirring testimony (2:20), "I have been crucified with Christ; and it is no longer I who live, but Christ lives in me; and the life which I now live in the flesh I live by faith in the Son of God, who loved me, and delivered Himself up for me." To them he had also outlined the foundations of victorious living and of spiritual growth (5:16-25). "Walk by the Spirit, and you will not carry out the desire of the flesh," he affirmed (5:16). He identified the morbid "deeds of the flesh," then the fragrant "fruit of the Spirit," summing up his advice, "Now those who belong to Christ Jesus have crucified the flesh"; and, "If we live by the Spirit, let us also walk by the Spirit" (vv. 24-25).

These would be the fundamental concepts upon which he would frame his profound letter to the church in Rome. See him expand on them, chapter by chapter.

It becomes evident that the purpose of this letter is to establish in proper sequence the fundamental doctrines of full salvation; that is, the universality of sinning; the blessedness of sins forgiven; the dreadful reality of indwelling sin as a principle even within the believer; the provision of deliverance from this indwelling sin; and the means for living an overcoming life—being "more than conquerors."

Now the doctrine of entire sanctification can be understood only when it is related to *sin*. This is not sin as a practice, generally known as "sins," but rather sin as a principle, as a part of the human nature. Paul, in the early chapters of Romans, deals with sins: first, as condemned, then as justified or forgiven. Thus he first deals with sins as *doing*—the practice of sinning (up to 5:11). He then undertakes in the following chapters to deal with sin as *being*, the principle of sin (5:12—8:39). He presents the doctrine of "Sin Revealed" in 5:12-21, and then of "Sin Overcome" in 6:1—8:39, which indeed is sanctification.

In reference to Paul's letter to the Romans, Dr. Alexander Maclaren declares:

> Some people say "give us the morality of the New Testament, never give us the theology!" But the apostle devotes the first eight chapters of his Epistle to building up the doctrinal structure of the Christian faith, tier after tier, before he attempts any exhortation to Christian duty. He would teach us by this that all the practical is to be built upon the doctrinal; that you cannot get morality without theology, unless you would like to have rootless flowers and lamps without oil. Practical holiness is not something that begins by *doing*, but by *being*.[1]

1. Sin is revealed, in chapters 5 through 8 *by name,* as *"sin."* It is in the singular, not *sins,* as in the earlier chapters. Furthermore, in a very marked fashion, which is not duplicated elsewhere in the Scriptures with the same consistency, this sin is identified in the Greek as "the" sin. See 5:12, 20, 21, and right on through 8:39. This article "the" is like a finger pointing, identifying, emphasizing. A study of the section will make it apparent that this is not *the* sin of stealing, of murder, of fornication, or of any other specific act. It is rather sin as a principle— "the sin principle." It is the principle of rebellion, of disobedience, of selfishness. It is a bent toward evil which indwells the heart. It is to this Paul directs his whole passage.

E. Stanley Jones says: "In carefully examining the New Testament doctrine of sin, Wesleyan scholars have found that Jesus, Paul and John clearly sustain the distinction between sin as a soul-current toward evil and sin as conduct into which men enter either by thought, word, or deed."[2]

Now this "soul-current toward evil" is variously termed original sin, Adamic sin, inbred sin. The Bible terms it the indwelling sin (Rom. 7:17-20); the "body of sin" (Rom. 6:6); "the body of this death" (Rom. 7:24); "the carnal mind" (Rom. 8:5-8, KJV; 1 Cor. 3:1-4); "the law of sin and of death" where law bears the meaning of controlling power (Rom. 7:21-25; 8:2).

It has been well said:

> The root principle of sin is seen to be self-will or self-centeredness. This preference for self-will instead of God's will is repeated in each successive generation. Self takes the place which belongs to God, and selfishness instead of the law of love becomes the rule of life. The outworking of this selfcenteredness can poison every human relationship and corrupts even such habits as were good in themselves. Thus man is born a sinner, with an inherited disposition to self-pleasing.[3]

2. Sin is revealed as to *its abode,* its dwelling place, its attachment. This sin principle of selfishness is an inherent characteristic of that which Paul calls "our old man" (Rom. 6:6, KJV; Eph. 4:22; Col. 3:9). God's treatment of sin and of the "old man" as explained by Paul will be examined in the next chapter.

But, as E. Stanley Jones says: "Our outer sins are rooted in something deeper. Just as my fingers are rooted in the palm of my hand, so my individual sins are rooted in the unsurrendered self."

3. Sin is revealed, again, as to *its entry into the world.* "Therefore, just as through one man sin entered into the world, and death through sin, and so death spread to all men, because all sinned" (Rom. 5:12). Since Adam was the head and representative of the human race, his sin affected the whole of mankind. For man is not only a distinct individual; he is a member of the human race, and, as such, inherits from his ancestors characteristics of many kinds. The principle of heredity affects the whole of human life, the transmission of Adam's sin being its earliest and farthest-reaching example.

4. Again, the principle of sin is revealed *as related to two men* and *to two distinct acts.* This is evident in Rom. 5:15, 17-18, and particularly in 19: "For as through the *one man's* disobedience the many were made sinners, even so through the obedience of *the One* the many will be made righteous." The curse came upon all by *the one act of disobedience;* God's grace is made available by *the one act of obedience.* Adam is recognized as an individual in a historic setting by Paul here, in 1 Cor. 15:22, 45; 1 Tim. 2:13-14; by Jude in verse 14; and by Jesus in Matt. 19:4, where "male" and "female" are singular; by Luke 3:38 in the lineage of Jesus.

Benjamin Field has helpfully commented:

> The relation of Adam to his descendents is not stated in the history of the fall. But the testimony of other parts of Scripture on this subject is so explicit that all attempts to evade it have been in vain. The point is proved by the parallel drawn by the Apostle between the first and the second Adam. The point of parallelism is noticed in general terms in Romans 5:14, where Adam is called, with evident allusion to his public representative character, "the figure", "type", or "model" of "Him that was to come"; and it is especially brought out in Rom. 5:18, 19 and 1 Cor. 15:22, 47.
>
> When Adam fell, involving his race in sorrow and pain, mercy revealed "the second Adam", through whom all might recover whatever they had lost through the first. This single consideration totally removes all reflections on the Divine justice or mercy, in making the state of all mankind so dependent on the behaviour of their common parent; for not one child of man finally loses thereby, unless by his own choice; and every one who receives "the grace of God in Christ" will be an unspeakable gainer.[4]

5. It was Jesus who pointed out yet another aspect of the revelation of sin—that *the very principle of sin is found in man's heart,* that man's heart is naturally sin-filled. In view of his dealing with the sin question it is not

unreasonable to believe that Paul was well aware of our Lord's statement. "That which proceeds out of the man," said Jesus, "that is what defiles the man. For from within, out of the heart of men, proceed the evil thoughts," He continued, thoughts of "fornications, thefts, murders, adulteries . . . sensuality, envy, slander, pride and foolishness. All these evil things *proceed from within* and defile the man" (Mark 7:20-23). Thus man's inner nature, his very heart, needs cleansing.

Since the sin principle is so deep-seated, it requires a basic, drastic approach if it is to be conquered.

> *Jesus, Thy fullness give;*
> *My soul and body bless.*
> *Cleanse me from sin, that I may live*
> *The life of holiness.*

9

*What Paul said
to the "beloved of God in Rome"*

On Being Crucified with Christ

ROMANS 6

John Wesley's great contribution to theology, that sanctification is a separate and subsequent work of grace, is apparently based largely on Paul's letter to the Romans. Man is *guilty* of his own personal sins. For these he may be forgiven. This is entailed in the act of justification, God's work *for* men, the heart of which is forgiveness (Rom. 1:1—5:11).

But man is also *defiled* with sin as a principle which he inherited from Adam. For this he is not responsible. In other words, man is not responsible for being born with this sinful nature. But he is responsible for availing himself of God's provision in the atonement to meet this deficiency. This condition of a defiled heart requires a separate, a different, a subsequent work of grace, consisting of cleansing, deliverance, a dying out to sin. This is the act of entire sanctification, God's work done *in* him (Rom. 5:12—8:39).

Now while God is quite able to perform both works of grace simultaneously, yet His every work is done according to man's faith, and faith operates only according to light and a sense of need. Very seldom do these accompany a man's conversion. It is the old "law of readiness" in operation. One learns when he is ready; when he has a sense of need, of interest, of immediacy—not before.

How long a time shall there be then between the two works of grace? Canaan was an 11-day march from Sinai (Deut. 1:2), but the murmuring Israelites took 40 years to make it. Paul charged the six-months-old Thessalonian church, "This is the will of God, even your sanctification" (KJV). Jesus prayed for His disciples of not more than three years' standing, "Sanctify them through thy truth" (KJV). Pentecost then happened within two months. Several years after being saved were required by Brengle for his sanctification. Some of us have required even longer, some much less. Who can define how long?

For some a delay may be due to lack of light on the subject. For others it is plain rebellion, unwillingness. And *this* is dangerous. Certainly God can sanctify at once—and wills to do it. But sanctification will not occur until, with the poet, we can say:

> *"Come, O Spirit, come to sanctify*
> *All my body, mind, and will.*
> *Come, oh, come, and self now crucify;*
> *Let me henceforth be like Jesus."*

In the sixth chapter of Romans, Paul deals forthrightly with the overcoming of the inbred sin as being a death *to* sin.

1. This death to sin is, first of all, through a *baptism into Christ's death.*

> What shall we say then? Are we to continue in sin that grace might increase? May it never be! How shall we who died to sin still live in it? Or do you not know that all of us who have been baptized into Christ Jesus have been baptized into His death? Therefore we have been buried with Him through baptism into death, in order that as Christ was raised from the dead through the glory of the Father, so we too might walk in new-

ness of life. For if we have become united with Him in the likeness of His death, certainly we shall be also in the likeness of His resurrection *(Rom. 6:1-5).*

He who is so baptized does not "continue in sin" nor does he "still live in it." Note that Paul does not say "continue *to* sin." The freedom which here is declared is not just from the *practice* of sinning (and it does include this), but from the very *principle* of sin. Neither does he say "baptized with water." Water is not a *means* of grace. But the Holy Spirit is (Eph. 4:4-6; Matt. 3:11; Luke 24:49; Acts 1:1-8). Also the passage implies that *there are believers who are not so baptized.* The word in v. 3 translated *"all of us who* have been baptized" is *hosoi,* a selective adjective, better translated as in the KJV, *"so many of us as* were baptized." It indicates that there is an alternate (see KJV in Rom. 2:12; 8:14; et al.). Some believers, unfortunately, have not so been baptized (by the Spirit). But all who have been so baptized have died to sin.

2. The death to sin is further likened to *crucifixion with Christ.*

Knowing this, that our old self [man] was crucified with Him, that our body of sin might be done away with, that we should no longer be slaves to sin; for he who has died is freed from sin *(Rom. 6:6-7).*

He who is so crucified does not "continue in sin," does not "still live in it." *Potentially* the "old self"—all we were before we were Christians when we were men in the flesh (the "man of old," the unsaved man with all his habits and desires)—was crucified with Christ at Calvary. But *experimentally* this is accomplished only when by faith and surrender we make it true.

It is just at this point that many a Christian falters. After conversion he discovers a new nature within, delighting in the law of God. But he learns, to his distress, that he *also* has an old nature, an "old man," the "old self," aroused, and battling for supremacy. Many Christians spend their lives in the seventh chapter of Romans or in Galatians 5. "For the good that I wish, I do not do; but I practice the very evil that I do not wish. . . . But I see a different law in the members of my body, waging war against the law of my mind, and making me a prisoner of the law of sin which is in my members" (Rom. 7:19, 23). "For the flesh sets its desire against the Spirit, and the Spirit against the flesh; for these are in opposition to one another, so that you may not do the things that you please" (Gal. 5:17). Yes, too many believers live a life of internal conflict *when they need not!* If they will present their "old self," their "old man" (Rom. 6:6), "the flesh" (Gal. 5:24) for crucifixion, they may say with Paul, "I am crucified with Christ" (Gal. 2:20, KJV).

The Salvation Army Handbook of Doctrine expresses it:

> Believers must do more than associate themselves with Calvary as those who look upon the Sin-bearer who suffers there *for* them. They are called to identify themselves with Him on the cross, as being crucified themselves *with* Him and fully united with Him, and He with them, so that His death means *the death of their old nature,* leading to a new life in the power of the Resurrection.[1]

Dean Alford declared: "St. Paul could never have said, 'I am crucified with Christ; it is no longer I that live, but Christ liveth in me' had self been still alive disputing with Christ the throne of the soul. Self had been nailed to the cross, and Christ had taken the supreme place in his soul."

Roy S. Nicholson has further analyzed this very helpfully:

> Not only is sin no essential part of our humanity, but also human nature, as God constituted it, is no barrier to holiness:

1. Man possessed a human nature before he possessed a carnal nature.

2. Man, while possessing a human nature, became possessed of a carnal nature which is not part of the original nature. . . .

4. Man may, by Christ's atoning death, be delivered or purged from the carnal nature, yet retain his human nature.[2]

This crucifixion of self will serve a twofold purpose (v. 6): "that our body of sin might be made powerless" (margin), and "that we should no longer be slaves to sin." Sin as a dominating principle within—the total body of sin—will become ineffectual, and therefore will no longer be the master of our lives.

"Some Christians who realize their justification before God," Talbot said, "are still under the power of sin. Every believer has been saved from the *guilt* of sin, but how few have been saved from the *power* of sin. God's plan is that we die out to sin."[3]

But note through it all that it is the "I" which dies, not sin *per se*. Paul, in declaring his crucifixion, immediately announced the newness and fullness of his life: "Christ lives in me," he cried. Can we not take warning from our Lord's parable of the sad fate of the *unoccupied* heart which, though "swept and put in order" (Luke 11:24-26), was not immune to contamination?

Charles Wesley helps us with:

> *Let earth no more my heart divide;*
> *With Christ may I be crucified*
> *And to thyself aspire.*
> *Dead to the world and all its toys,*
> *Its idle pomp and fading joys,*
> *Be Thou my one desire.*

3. Sin as a principle in our lives is overcome by *faith* (v. 8; Acts 15:9). History records a long series of experi-

ments by man to become holy by his own efforts. He has tried legalism that includes asceticism, martyrdom, and monasticism. He has tried emotionalism, which was first evident in the church at Corinth. He has attempted to accomplish holiness through the church in sacramentalism, ceremonialism, scholasticism, and ritualism. He has attempted it through the "deeper life" efforts of mysticism and pietism. But God ordered it that sanctification would be accomplished "by faith in Me," that is, in the atoning sacrifice (Eph. 5:25-27; Heb. 13:12).

It might be well at this point to pause long enough to review Paul's commission as received on the Damascus road nearly a quarter of a century prior to this letter. Luke reports in Acts, undoubtedly as he had heard Paul declare it many times:

"I heard a voice. . . . And the Lord said, 'I am Jesus whom you are persecuting. But arise, and stand on your feet; for this purpose I have appeared to you, to appoint you a minister and a witness not only to the things which you have seen, but also to the things in which I will appear to you; delivering you from the Jewish people and from the Gentiles, to whom I am sending you, to open their eyes so that they may turn from darkness to light and from the dominion of Satan to God, in order that they may receive *forgiveness of sins and an inheritance among those who have been sanctified by faith* in Me'" *(Acts 26:14-18).*

Paul never forgot that divine appointment to proclaim a dual message: *the forgiveness of sins,* and *sanctification by faith.*

As Luther had proclaimed salvation by faith alone (Eph. 2:8), so John Wesley proclaimed sanctification by faith alone (Acts 15:9). Sanctification and holy living thus were removed from the cloister, the abbey, the monastery, the church itself, and placed in the street, the workshop, the home, the heart of the humble believer. There was no requirement of profound knowledge, impractical works, unattainable seclusion, but rather of simple faith in the Lord's finished atonement. This included not only the forgiveness of sins, but also the deliverance from the very principle of sin.

4. Sin is also overcome by a *daily acceptance* of the fact of sanctification: "Even so consider yourselves to be dead to sin, but alive to God in Christ Jesus" (6:11). If faith makes *real* the life of holiness, an active acceptance of the fact makes it *practical.* And the acceptance is twofold. There is the negative fact of being "dead to sin," but also the positive fact of being "alive to God in Christ Jesus." Sanctification is not only the removal of that which destroys, but also the addition of that which constructs.

5. Now the *kind* of action indicated should be noted. The tense of "died" (v. 2), "baptized" (v. 3), "crucified" (v. 6), "made powerless" (v. 6, margin) is *aorist,* the tense of a specific occurrence or event. Again, there is agreement with our Lord's petition, "Sanctify them"—at a moment's time (John 17:17)—and the Pentecostal experience of "suddenly." There is the decisiveness of the Pentecostal experience. However, the tense of the verb "consider" (v. 11) is *present,* in agreement with our Lord's prayer "that they themselves also may *be* sanctified in truth" (John 17:19). This is the tense which indicates action which persists in an unbroken, continued, moment-by-moment train, which indeed defines a *life* of holiness. Day by day "consider yourselves to be dead to sin, but alive to God in Christ Jesus" (v. 11).

> *Come, O Spirit, come to sanctify*
> *All my body, mind, and will.*
> *Come, oh, come, and self now crucify;*
> *Let me henceforth be like Jesus.*

10

*What Paul said
to the church in Rome about being*

More than Conquerors

ROMANS 7—8

In chapter 6 of his letter to the Romans, Paul presented the act of sanctification as death to sin through a baptism of the Spirit, through crucifixion of the old self, by faith, and the life of holiness as a daily acceptance of the holy life. In the latter part of chapter 7 and the early part of chapter 8 he now presents the experience of sanctification as a deliverance from sin through *substitution*—the substitution of a higher law for a lower one.

1. He considers first *the struggle within.* Picturing himself as a carnal, self-centered Christian who finds himself sold under the sin principle, he finally, in a word of personal testimony, declares his deliverance. Here the Mosaic law is identified by a capital L in the NASB. The passage is Rom. 7:14-20. It declares the *fact,* the terrible reality of the struggle.

> For we know the Law is spiritual; but I am of flesh, sold into bondage to sin. For that which I am doing, I do not understand; for I am not practicing what I would like to do, but I am doing the very things I hate. But if I do the very thing I do not wish to do, I agree with the Law, confessing that it is good. So now, no longer am I the one doing it, but sin which indwells me. For I know that nothing good dwells in me, that is, in my flesh; for the wishing is present in me, but the doing of the

good is not. For the good that I wish, I do not do; but I practice the very evil that I do not wish. But if I am doing the very thing I do not wish, I am no longer the one doing it, but sin which dwells in me.

Continuing, Paul next identifies the *cause* of the struggle. Note that "law" is no longer a divine commandment, spelled with a capital *L*, but a governing principle, a controlling power (like the law of gravity or the law of inertia), spelled with a small *l*. In fact there are *two* embattled laws or principles. Victory comes through the ascension of the law or controlling principle of the Spirit over the law or controlling principle of sin. Hear Paul describe in vivid terms the cause of the struggle and how it was resolved.

First, he speaks of the cause:

I find then the principle that evil is present in me, the one who wishes to do good. For I joyfully concur with the law of God in the inner man, but I see a different law in the members of my body, waging war against the law of my mind, and making me a prisoner of the law of sin which is in my members. Wretched man that I am! Who will set me free from this body of death? *(7:21-24).*

Now he speaks of the *resolution* of that struggle within:

Thanks be to God through Jesus Christ our Lord! So then, on the one hand I myself with my mind am serving the law of God, but on the other, with my flesh, the law of sin. There is therefore now no condemnation for those who are in Christ Jesus. For the law of the Spirit of life in Christ Jesus has set you free from the law of sin and of death *(7:25—8:2)*

"The compulsive power of a new affection" Chalmers calls it.

The songwriter has expressed it:

Though great the world's attractions be,
I pass contented by;

> *Gladly I sacrifice their charms*
> *For those enjoyed on high.*

The story is told in the *Odyssey* of the alluring sirens who sang so beautifully on the shore rocks that the sailors would steer the ship in their direction and be shipwrecked. Captains of the vessels tried in vain to turn them from their purpose. One put cotton in the sailors' ears to keep out the sound. Another lashed them to the mast. But many ships continued to be lost. Ulysses, however, solved the problem by securing the services of Orpheus, who presented better, more alluring music than the sirens. The sailors lost their interest in the sirens, who, in despair, cast themselves into the sea and became rocks.

So it is that, when allowed to rule, the higher law of the Spirit utterly defeats the lower law of sin and death.

2. In progressing from the seventh to the eighth chapter, it is apparent that the life of holiness is the triumph of the "Spirit" of chapter 8 over the "I" of chapter 7. In the earlier chapter, "I" and its derivatives appear no fewer than 38 times, but only 3 times in the latter. In the seventh, "Spirit" or "spiritual" do not appear at all. But in the victorious eighth chapter, where "I" all but disappears, the Spirit takes over, with no fewer than 23 appearances.

Further, he who lives for *self* will live under bondage. He who lives in and under *the Spirit* will live "set . . . free from the body of this death" (8:1-13). Jesus, indeed, had said, "If anyone wishes to come after me, let him deny himself."

3. Let us look more closely at this remarkable eighth chapter. Chapter 3 had dealt with God *declaring* the repentant sinner righteous. Chapter 8 deals with God *making* the believer holy. The one chapter deals with Christ's work *for* the *sinner* in justification; the other deals with His work *in* the *believer* unto sanctification. In addition,

chapter 8 emphasizes the Spirit's part in sanctification, while chapter 6 presents the believer's part.

This unparalleled chapter takes us from the "no condemnation" of verse 1 to the "no separation" of verse 39. It takes us out of the utter despair of "O wretched man that I am, who shall deliver me?" (KJV) to the glorious conquest of being "more than conquerors" (KJV). The brilliance of God's Holy Spirit illuminates His truth, and in turn illuminates the soul of him who will subject himself to the presence, the possession, and the power of the Holy Spirit.

In this eighth chapter, the life of overcoming, of the truly sanctified life, is declared possible through the action of the triune God.

It is possible first for those who appropriate the provision of *the Holy Spirit:*

> And in the same way the Spirit also helps our weakness; for we do not know how to pray as we should, but the Spirit Himself intercedes for us with groanings too deep for words; and He who searches the hearts knows what the mind of the Spirit is, because He intercedes for the saints according to the will of God *(Rom. 8:26-27).*

The life of overcoming is possible also to those whose love to Him is unbroken (note that "love" is in the present tense), through the provision of *the Father.*

> And we know that God causes all things to work together for good to those who love God, to those who are the called according to His purpose. For whom He foreknew, He also predestined to become conformed to the image of His Son, that He might be the first-born among many brethren; and whom He predestined, these He also called; and whom He called, these He also justified; and whom He justified, these He also glorified.
>
> What then shall we say to these things? If God is for us, who is against us? He who did not spare His own Son, but delivered Him up for us all, how will He not

also with Him freely give us all things? Who will bring a charge against God's elect? God is the one who justifies *(8:28-33)*.

Again, this truly sanctified life is possible for those who are truly justified, through the provision of *the Son*.

Who is the one who condemns? Christ Jesus is He who died, yes, rather who was raised, who is at the right hand of God, who also intercedes for us *(8:34)*.

Finally, this victorious life is possible through the triumph of *the believer himself,* as he finds himself surrounded by the security of God's love:

Who shall separate us from the love of Christ? Shall tribulation, or distress, or persecution, or famine, or nakedness, or peril, or sword? Just as it is written: "FOR THY SAKE WE ARE BEING PUT TO DEATH ALL DAY LONG; WE WERE CONSIDERED SHEEP TO BE SLAUGHTERED." But in all these things we overwhelmingly conquer through Him who loved us. For I am convinced that neither death, nor life, nor angels, nor principalities, nor things present, nor things to come, nor powers, nor height, nor depth, nor any other created thing, shall be able to separate us from the love of God, which is in Christ Jesus our Lord *(8:35-39)*.

4. Be it noted again in this eighth chapter that the *acquisition* of this victorious life is expressed in the aorist tense, the tense of a simple occurrence: "For the law of the Spirit of life in Christ Jesus *has set you free* from the law of sin and of death" (8:2). Paul remembered the day, probably the hour, when it happened. However, the *enjoyment,* the *living* of this victorious life is governed by the present tense of continuous or recurrent action. These verbs are: "helps" (v. 26), "intercedes" (v. 26), "causes" (v. 28), "who love God" (v. 28), "who are [being] called" (v. 28), "freely give" (v. 32), "intercedes" (v. 34), "overwhelmingly conquer" (v. 37). All these suggest uninterrupted, progressive sanctification, the *life* of holiness.

Thus, in this sweeping doctrinal section of Romans,

Paul has brought together the teaching of his Lord, the experience of the Early Church (Jews and Gentiles alike), and his own writings to the churches at Thessalonica, at Corinth, and at Galatia. He has matched these with the experience of the disciples on the Day of Pentecost and in the years which had followed. And, under the moving of the Holy Spirit, he has given to Christendom a profoundly convincing document on sins, salvation, sin, and sanctification.

William Booth caught something of Paul's spirit when he penned:

Singing, I feel I shall conqueror be.
  Victory for me!
Boundless salvation is coming to me.
  Victory for me!
Cleansed by Thy blood, I shall walk in the light;
Held in Thine arms, I shall live in Thy sight;
Filled with Thy love, I shall win in the fight.
  Victory for me!

Finished my work, I shall mount to the skies.
  Victory for me!
Comrades and kindred will shout as I rise.
  Victory for me!
Then saints and angels their welcomes will sing;
Then in His glory I'll see my great King;
Then in loud rapture I'll make heaven ring.
  Victory for me!

11

*What Paul wrote
to "all who are beloved of God in Rome" about*

Transformed Christians

ROMANS 12—15

> I beseech you therefore, brethren, by the mercies of God, that ye present your bodies a living sacrifice, holy, acceptable unto God, which is your reasonable service. And be not conformed to this world: but be ye transformed by the renewing of your mind, that ye may prove what is that good, and acceptable, and perfect, will of God *(Rom. 12:1-2, KJV).*

The "therefore" with which Paul opens this section of his Epistle reaches a long way back. Painstakingly and in great detail he has laid the foundation of doctrine upon which a Christian can not only place his faith, but also build his life. His "therefore" reaches back to the beginning of the Epistle. In the light of those doctrinal principles previously enunciated, he is now ready to outline the facts of practical, godly living that establishes Christians as "more than conquerors" (KJV). As the goal of redemption was shown to be not only justification but also sanctification, so the ethics of the God-kind of righteousness is not only the forgiveness of the past, but also the establishment of a present life of holiness.

These two verses call for Christians to "prove what is that good, and acceptable, and perfect, will of God" through a decisive dedication, a consistent separation, and a continuing transformation.

1. The will of God varies for individuals regarding many things. Their health, their mates (thank the Lord), and other matters of daily living are different in God's plan for them. But "that good, and acceptable, and perfect, will of God" is something else. It is universal, unchanging, encompassing all mankind. And it is twofold. Paul has carefully established that fact in this Epistle. God's universal will is first that a man be justified, and then that he be sanctified. Paul has affirmed this in other letters as well. In his first letter to Timothy, chapter 2, he writes: "This is good and acceptable in the sight of God our Savior, *who desires all men to be saved* and to come to the knowledge of the truth." (See also 2 Pet. 3:9.) Then, to the Thessalonians he had declared, "For this is the will of God, *your sanctification."* It is apparent then, that that "good, and acceptable, and perfect, will of God" here refers to this twofold purpose of the atonement—that men may be saved and sanctified. This complete plan is sometimes referred to as "full salvation." *This is God's will for all.*

2. The *means for implementing* this will of God are threefold:

a. The first is a precise act of dedication. This act includes several things. It is *voluntary,* as indicated in the verb "present." This is comparable to the giving of a gift. It is not forced or compulsory but is a willing act of love. Again, it is *personal*—"your bodies." No one can call upon the resources of another, or purchase a gift to be presented. It is yourself which God wants most. This will include your skill, your strength, your everyday living, your habits. This can be very challenging, and very practical, to "prove" His will.

Again, this gift is *sacrificial.* To the Hebrew of that day a sacrifice to God was a very important part of worship. Abraham had set the standard of sacrificial giving when he offered his own beloved son. A Hebrew family was sacrificial when it offered its best, most nearly perfect lamb. God marked the peak of sacrificial giving when He presented His only begotten, beloved Son.

Furthermore, this gift is to be both *living* and *holy.* It is the *life* God can use, the *life* through which He can present himself to the world. But it must be a holy life, a holy body. This dedication is not the act of sanctification. That has been called for in chapters 6 through 8. This is the act of presenting the sanctified life and the holy body to Him.

Again, this is to be an act of reasonable "worship." "Service" in the New Testament can be "doing" *(diakonia)* as with Martha in Luke 10:40. Or, as here, it can be "worshipping" *(latreia).* (See Luke 1:74.) Paul here identifies the act of dedication as a sacred act of worship. This spirit is aptly caught by Brindley Boon in his song:

> *Time, health, and talents presenting,*
> *All that I have shall be Thine;*
> *Heart, mind, and will consecrating,*
> *No longer shall they be mine.*
>
> *Take Thou my life, Lord,*
> *In deep submission I pray,*
> *My all to Thee dedicating.*
> *Accept my offering today.*

Finally, it is a *decisive* gift. The verb "present" is in the aorist tense of a specific act. The dedication must be complete and final.

b. The second means for implementing the will of God is a consistent separation: "Do not be conformed to this world," or "to this age." Now the word "conformed" delineates the assuming of an outward appearance contrary to the inward life. This masquerade is entirely foreign to the Christian witness.

Worldliness is often defined in terms of clothes, hair, places of amusement, and so forth. But here the emphasis is on *this* age, the temporal age, as compared to *that* age, the eternal age. Thus worldliness has certain aspects.

Worldliness is the spirit that says, *"This* is the age that is important. Indeed, there may not be another age at all. So live it up. 'Eat, drink, and be merry, for tomorrow you will die.'" There is no eternal tomorrow. Again it says, *"This* is the age of self-sufficiency in mind, will, morals," disavowing man's lost condition and the need of man's repentance, faith, surrender, and of God's mercy and grace. *"This* is the age of self-pleasing," not allowing for self-denial, self-restraint. Worldliness is the spirit that, at its best, says, *"This* is the age we must serve humanity and improve the world," forgetting that our first duty and first love must be to God. It substitutes man-made goodness for godliness.

These are some of the earmarks of the worldliness of which Paul would warn the Christian. And that this must be a constant vigilance is indicated by the continuing *present* tense of "do not be conformed."

c. Proving God's will, moreover, requires a continuous transformation: "Be transformed." It must be realized that the Greek verb *metamorphoō* is used but three times in the Scriptures. In speaking of Jesus, Matthew says: "And He *was transfigured* before them; and His face shone like the sun, and His garments became as white as light" (17:2). Of this Peter later said, "We were eyewitnesses of His majesty"; and John declared, "We beheld His glory, glory as of the only begotten from the Father, full of grace and truth." Of the Christian, Paul had said to the Corinthians, "But we all, with unveiled face beholding as in a mirror the glory of the Lord, *are being transformed* into the same image from glory to glory, just as from the Lord, the Spirit" (2 Cor. 3:18). And now Paul exhorts all Christians, through those at Rome, to "be *transformed* by the renewing of your mind."

Not that it is to be a sudden transformation, as apparently it was in the Saviour (when the aorist tense was used). His was a disclosure of the glory already present within. Paul uses the continuing present tense, both in his letter to the Corinthians ("are being transformed") and here ("be [day by day, moment by moment] transformed"). This is to be a continuous transformation. This the child of God will accomplish by faithfully "beholding as in a mirror the glory of the Lord," whereupon he will constantly be transformed "just as from the Lord, the Spirit." Man must consistently direct his gaze, his thoughts, his hungers; God the Holy Spirit will then do the transforming, day by day, moment by moment.

Was it something of this which his persecutors saw when Stephen was brought before them? "And fixing their gaze on him, all who were sitting in the Council saw his face like the face of an angel" (Acts 6:15).

3. And what does it mean to *"prove"* this ultimate, this supreme will of God—namely, our full salvation?

The Greek word *dokimadzo* has an element of *discernment,* as in Luke 12:56, "You hypocrites! You know how to analyze the appearance of the earth and the sky, but why do you not analyze this present time?" In a real sense the three steps already listed will help the Christian to analyze or discern God's great will.

The word also has an element of *testing,* in the hope and expectation that the test will prove successful, as in 1 Pet. 1:7: "That the proof of your faith, being more precious than gold which is perishable, even though tested by fire, may be found to result in praise and glory and honor at the revelation of Jesus Christ." His fulfillment of the three requirements Paul outlines will enable the Christian to approach the testing of the "good, and acceptable, and perfect," will of God for him, in the hope and expectation that the test will prove successful.

The word also has an element of *proving* to himself and to the world *by demonstration,* practice, and experience the entirely practical element of the life of holiness. Indeed, it would seem that it is to this that Paul applies himself in the chapters of this section of the letter which follow.

Furthermore, "prove" is in the present, persistent tense. Paul is saying that "you may prove"—not once for all, but again and again, day by day—the "good, and acceptable, and perfect, will of God." Sanctified Christians should consistently demonstrate this holy living.

In the balance of his letter Paul then enumerates the many *to whom* this sanctified life should be manifested. It should be demonstrated:

a. To the Church—in diversified unity (12:3-8)

b. To fellow believers—in love (12:9-13)

c. To the world—in kindly affection (12:14-21)

d. To the state—in respect (13:1-7)

e. To society—in practical righteousness (13:8-14)

f. To weak brethren—in compassion (14:1—15:7)

A study of this concluding phase of Paul's letter in this light can be most rewarding and challenging.

Thus Paul expresses the culmination, the practical climax of the Epistle's theme: "The just shall *live* by faith" (1:17, KJV); and his further exposition of this life of faith: "Nay, in all these things we are more than conquerors through him that loved us" (8:37, KJV).

As Roy L. Laurin says:

> Here we find that duty follows doctrine; responsibility follows revelation; and practice follows principle. Unless these things appear in the course and conduct of

our daily living, we give the lie to our faith. Their absence tells us that the presence of Christianity in us is only a fiction and a pretense. "All our professions, our desires, our ideals, our hopes, our intentions will count for nothing unless we manifest holiness in thought, word, and deed in all the circles of daily life and activity." Here is the fact of privilege following precept. And we must remember with care that Christianity contains the preaching of privilege as well as precept.[1]

The poet has given us the searching prayer:

If on my soul a trace of sin remaineth,
  If on my hands a stain may yet be seen,
If one dark thought a wearied mind retaineth,
  Oh, wash me, Lord, till every part be clean.

For I would live that men may see thyself in me;
  I would in faith ascend Thy holy hill,
And with my thoughts in tune with Thy divinity,
  Would learn how best to do Thy holy will.

12

*What Paul said
to the "saints . . . at Ephesus" about being*

Chosen to Be Holy

EPHESIANS 1—3

Purposeful living! There is nothing that enriches life more than purpose. How tedious, how meaningless, how disheartening can be a life spent in aimless movement from this to that!

One of the great blessings of the Christian's life is that he is chosen for a purpose, called with an end in view; "chosen to be holy."

There are four letters in the third group of Paul's Epistles—Ephesians, Philippians, Colossians, and Philemon—written about A.D. 62 or 63 from the prison in Rome. (See Appendix V, "Chronology of the New Testament.") Unhurried, and without the day-by-day pressure of his ministry to churches, his preaching and travelling, they represent Paul's mature thinking. They include his final word on doctrine, particularly in Ephesians. Though among Paul's later writings, they still predate the books of all other New Testament authors with the possible exception of James.

There is substantial evidence that Ephesians was not directed particularly to the church in that city, but was rather a circular letter written for all the churches of Asia. A marginal note says, "Some ancient manuscripts omit *at Ephesus.*" It may well be that our Book of Ephesians was taken from that copy of the letter which was sent to the mother church at Ephesus, the capital of the province of Asia.

Now, if it is true that Romans represents the peak of Paul's writings regarding man's sinfulness and God's remedy for sin, Ephesians must take its place of greatness in recording God's eternal plan *that His people should be holy*. The letter constitutes God's great call to holy living.

> Blessed be the God and Father of our Lord Jesus Christ, who has blessed us with every spiritual blessing in the heavenly places in Christ, just as *He chose us in Him before the foundation of the world, that we should be holy and blameless before Him* (Eph. 1:3-4).

These two verses, in Greek, are but the beginning of a long sentence extending through verse 14. In the English translations there are several sentences in this passage. These two verses stand on their own as a complete thought, while the remainder of the passage completes the sentence with modifying phrases and statements grammatically and theologically dependent upon this first part.

Indeed, Paul wraps the whole Epistle up in this theme when, near the end, he repeats it in identical words. Referring to believers as "the church" he declares:

> Christ also loved the church and gave Himself up for her; that He might sanctify her, having cleansed her by the washing of water with the word, that He might present to Himself the church in all her glory, having no spot or wrinkle or any such thing; but *that she should be holy and blameless (5:25-27).*

To this premier "spiritual blessing in the heavenly places in Christ" (v. 3) are added, in verses 5 through 14, the related and supporting blessings of adoption (v. 5), grace (v. 6), redemption (v. 7), forgiveness of sins (v. 7), an inheritance (vv. 11-12), and a sealing by the Holy Spirit (v. 13). Together they constitute "every spiritual blessing."

1. Let us again examine the central theme of the Epistle (v. 4):
   a. The time—"before the foundation of the world"
   b. The action—God "chose us in Him"
   c. The purpose—in order that His people should,
      (1) regarding character, be "holy"
      (2) regarding conduct, be "blameless"
   d. The appraisal—"before Him"

Thus the tone is set for the whole Epistle.

"For this reason" Paul mounts an earnest prayer for believers (1:15-23): that through an experiential, personal knowledge of God they might have wisdom and revelation; that through being enlightened they may comprehend something of "the hope of His calling" and of "the riches of the glory" that by inheritance is theirs. He reminds them that these are possible through the same power exhibited by God in raising Christ from the grave and in exalting Him to His place of incomparable authority and honor.

Paul then deals straightforwardly with the *new life* needed by, and available to, Jew and Gentile alike (2:1-10) if he is to *live* the *holy life* God requires. This comes by being "made . . . alive together with Christ." In the next paragraph (2:11-22) he urgently reminds his Gentile readers that, though previously exiles to the promises of God, they now were one with Israel in all these promises. "But now in Christ Jesus you who formerly were far off have been brought near by the blood of Christ" (v. 13).

"For this reason I Paul [am] the prisoner of Christ Jesus for the sake of you Gentiles," he continues in 3:1-13. He identifies the fact that the Gentiles are now fellow heirs of the gospel as "the mystery of Christ," of which mystery he is made a minister. And all this was "in accordance with the *eternal purpose* which He carried out in Christ Jesus our Lord."

2. Having established these important facts, Paul then returns to the original theme of his Epistle (3:14-21).

"For this reason"—because you were called to be holy—he declares, "I bow my knees before the Father, from whom every family in heaven and on earth derives its name." He then identifies the ultimate goal for followers of Christ. In five great petitions, Paul reveals something of "the inheritance" of the "sanctified" which he had been charged to proclaim (Acts 26:18). He earnestly prays:

a. For spiritual *power* for believers—"That He would grant you, according to the riches of His glory, to be strengthened with power through His Spirit in the inner man" (v. 16). As power was Christ's first promise to His disciples (Acts 1:8), so power is Paul's first petition for his people. This strengthening is not to be *from* the riches of His glory, but *according to* those riches. It is said that John D. Rockefeller used to toss out dimes to see people scramble for them. This would have been *from* his riches. Later he established great foundations with substantial gifts. This was *according to* his riches.

b. For spiritual *permanence* to all believers—"So that Christ may dwell in your hearts through faith" (v. 17). The verb is a perfective form of the usual verb "to dwell," indicating a permanence—"may settle." Christ should not be a visitor but the Proprietor.

c. For spiritual *provision*—"That you, being rooted and grounded in love" (v. 17). Adam Clarke notes that Paul reinforces his prayer for their provision by the use of a double metaphor—"rooted and grounded." As trees, they are to be "rooted in love," the soil in which their souls are to grow. As a building, they are to be "grounded in love," the foundation upon which their souls are firm and unshakable.

d. For spiritual *perception*—"That you . . . may be able to comprehend with all the saints what is the breadth and length and height and depth, and to know the love of Christ which surpasses knowledge" (vv. 18-19). Four dimensions of His love! The breadth of His mercy, the length of His long-suffering, the height of His holiness, the depth of sin to which His love will reach. And this is a paradox—to gain the knowledge which is really unattainable by human perception.

e. For spiritual *plentitude*—"That you may be filled up to all the fulness of God" (v. 19). Now in Christ "all the fulness of Deity dwells in bodily form" (Col. 2:9). And *He* comes to dwell within us. What a challenging thought, that the believer may thus be "filled with all the fulness" of Deity—so there is room for none else! Even as the smallest cup can be filled with the "fulness" of the waters of the sea—until it brims over! For this Paul prayed.

For this Francis Bottome prayed:

> *Come, Holy Ghost, all-sacred Fire!*
> *Come, fill this earthly temple now,*
> *Emptied of every base desire.*
> *Reign Thou within, and only Thou.*
>
> *Fill every chamber of my soul;*
> *Fill all my thoughts, my passions fill,*
> *Till under Thy supreme control,*
> *Submissive, rests my cheerful will.*

Paul knew that the fulfillment of such "an inheritance among those who have been sanctified by faith" would enable Gentile and Jew alike to live "holy and blameless before Him."

It was in such a spirit of confidence that he closed with the incomparable benediction:

Now to Him who is able to do exceeding abundantly beyond all that we ask or think, according to the power that works within us, to Him be the glory in the church and in Christ Jesus to all generations forever and ever. Amen *(vv. 20-21)*.

In this first portion of the Epistle, Paul has outlined the *call* of the Christian *unto* a holy life. In the portion to follow he deals with the *walk* of the Christian *in* a holy life.

Believe Him! Believe Him! The Holy One is waiting
To perfect within you what grace has begun.
God wills for His people an uttermost salvation;
To sanctify you wholly the Spirit will come.
—ALBERT ORSBORN

13

*What Paul said
to "the saints . . . at Ephesus" concerning*

The Holy Walk

EPH. 4:1—5:17

It is one thing *to be chosen* in order that we should be holy and blameless, as outlined in the first portion of the Epistle, and another thing *to practice* that holy life in deed and in fact. In this second portion of his Epistle, Paul exhorts repeatedly to that life in the terms of a "walk."

The "therefores" of 4:1, 17 and 5:1 mark three exhortations, each of which refers back to the entire first three chapters, but especially to God's call to holy living, "that we should be holy and blameless before Him," and to that prayer "that you may be filled up to all the fulness of God." Let us examine these exhortations in order.

1. Paul's first exhortation is to a *worthy* walk. "I, therefore, the prisoner of the Lord, entreat you to walk in a manner worthy of the calling with which you have been called" (4:1). This calling to holiness is not for future ages in eternity; it is for *now,* for the *present,* for *today.* Paul then delineates four elements of that worthy walk, elements which apply to this present, everyday life.

a. First, the walk should be characterized by *humility.* "With all humility and gentleness, with patience, showing forbearance to one another in love" (v. 2). Holiness is not exhibited in pride. Well might Paul remember the account which Jesus gave of the Pharisee who stood in the Temple, making boasts of his own religious perfection (holiness) and casting aspersions on the tax gatherer with his shortcomings. Meanwhile the tax gatherer was beating his breast, saying, "God, be merciful to me, *the* sinner!" Of them Jesus said, "Every one who exalts himself shall be humbled, but he who humbles himself shall be exalted." Indeed, said Paul, humility is an essential element in a worthy walk.

b. Again, the walk should be characterized by *harmony.* "Being diligent to preserve the unity of the Spirit in the bond of peace" (v. 3). Immediately in succeeding verses (4-6) he speaks of *one* body, *one* Spirit, *one* hope, *one* Lord, *one* faith, *one* baptism, *one* God. Note parenthetically that "one hope *of your calling"* is right in the middle of these aspects of unity.

> Being diligent to preserve the unity of the Spirit in the bond of peace. There is one body and one Spirit, just as also you were called in one hope of your calling; one Lord, one faith, one baptism, one God and Father of all who is over all and through all and in all *(4:3-6).*

Divisiveness has no part in the walk of holiness. Again, Paul's mind might well return to the teaching of Jesus, which he would have heard from John. For in the very midst of His great prayer for His disciples Jesus repeatedly prayed for their unity (John 17:11, 21, 22, 23).

c. The worthy walk should also be characterized by *helpfulness.*

> But to each one of us grace was given according to the measure of Christ's gift. . . . And He gave some as apostles, and some as prophets, and some as evangelists, and some as pastors and teachers, for the equipping of the saints for the work of service, to the building up of the body of Christ *(4:7, 11-12).*

God endows His people with various gifts. And in the walk

of holiness God-given talents must be used to His honor and glory in the preparing of other Christians for their Christian service, and in the building up of the Church. There is no place for irresponsibility. There is no place for irritability with one another. Gifts differ. But all are to be respected, and used.

Along with all His public ministry, Jesus had laid great stress on the private instruction of His own chosen disciples for their work of service, each in his own sphere. Before sending them out on any mission He had spent long hours, in what is called the Sermon on the Mount, in careful instruction (Matthew 5—7). And before leaving them He gave the final hours of His ministry to His own in the Upper Room (John 13—17), that they might be equipped for their work as responsible individuals.

The holy walk is to be practical, useful, productive, cooperative.

d. Again, the walk should be characterized by that *holy growth* that climaxes in maturity: "Until we all attain to the unity of the faith, and of the knowledge of the Son of God, to a mature man, to the measure of the stature which belongs to the fulness of Christ" (4:13). Paul would not be ignorant of such parables of our Lord as that of the seed growing secretly (Mark 4:26-29) and of the mustard seed (vv. 30-32). Nor would he be unaware of the account His disciples gave of the boy Jesus himself: "And the Child continued to grow and become strong, increasing in wisdom; and the grace of God was upon Him. . . . And Jesus kept increasing in wisdom and stature, and in favor with God and men" (Luke 2:40, 52). No, in the walk of holiness there is no place for arrested maturity, for childishness of behavior, for smug satisfaction over present development. Holy living means constant growth.

2. Paul's next use of "therefore" contains *an exhorta-*

tion to cessation—"That you walk no longer just as the Gentiles also walk" (v. 17). This is followed by *an exhortation to restoration*—"Be renewed in the spirit of your mind" (v. 23).

The Ephesians *had* walked, and possibly to some extent were *still* walking, like unbelieving Gentiles. The example of the world is so easily emulated! "Everybody does it." This must cease. The renewal mentioned here is not that of the mind itself in its natural powers of memory, judgment, and perception, but "the *spirit* of your mind." This, under the controlling power of the indwelling Holy Spirit, directs the mind's bent and energies Godward. For the Gentiles it is "the futility of their mind." For God's children it is to be "the spirit of your mind."

These verbs, being in the present tense in the Greek, represent a pattern of life—one to be terminated ("cease following"), and the other to be perpetuated ("be constantly renewed").

> This I say therefore, and affirm together with the Lord, that you walk no longer just as the Gentiles also walk, in the futility of their mind, being darkened in their understanding, excluded from the life of God, because of the ignorance that is in them, because of the hardness of their heart; and they, having become callous, have given themselves over to sensuality, for the practice of every kind of impurity with greediness.
>
> But you did not learn Christ in this way, if indeed you have heard Him and have been taught in Him, just as truth is in Jesus, that, in reference to your former manner of life, you lay aside the old self, which is being corrupted in accordance with the lusts of deceit, and that you be renewed in the spirit of your mind, and put on the new self, which in the likeness of God has been created in righteousness and holiness of the truth *(4:17-24).*

Note the passage also contains *a command to separation*—"lay aside the old self"; then *a directive to acquisi-*

tion—"and put on the new self." These commands are in the aorist tense. They call for decisive action, to be done at once and once for all. (See Appendix regarding the significance of tense *changes*.) In Romans, Paul identified the old self (the old man) as being crucified, here as being laid aside. In both cases the acts are decisive. A decision has to be made to become a member of the body of Christ—"You must be born again." A decision must also be made if one is to be enabled "to walk in a manner worthy of the calling with which you have been called"—"lay aside," "was crucified," "put on."

In the verses which follow (4:25-32), Paul is setting forth the *principles of righteousness and holiness* that relate to the new man, which "in the likeness of God has been created in righteousness and holiness of the truth."

a. The principle of *truth:* "Laying aside falsehood, SPEAK TRUTH, EACH ONE of you, WITH HIS NEIGHBOR, for we are members of one another" (v. 25).

b. The principle of *self-control:* "BE ANGRY, AND YET DO NOT SIN; do not let the sun go down on your anger, and do not give the devil an opportunity" (vv. 26-27). Be it noted this is not the sudden anger of uncontrolled temper, *thumos* (Matt. 2:16), but rather the settled indignation of the wrath of reason, *orgē* (Rom. 1:18). Through this admonition Paul would say: "Let your anger be toward that which hurts *others,* never at that which wounds *you.* And don't perpetuate your annoyance, irritation [*parorgismos*]."

c. The principle of *industry*: "Let him who steals steal no longer; but rather let him labor, performing with his own hands what is good, in order that he may have something to share with him who has need" (v. 28). And with industry he would blend responsibility, generosity.

d. The principle of *proper use of the tongue:*

Let no unwholesome word proceed from your mouth, but only such a word as is good for edification according to the need of the moment, that it may give grace to those who hear. And do not grieve the Holy Spirit of God, by whom you were sealed for the day of redemption. Let all bitterness and wrath and anger and clamor and slander be put away from you, along with all malice *(vv. 29-31).*

e. The principle of *graciousness:* "And be kind to one another, tender-hearted, forgiving each other, just as God in Christ also has forgiven you" (v. 32).

3. Once more Paul refers back to his theme with a "therefore," and then uses the figure of "walk," this time in a series. He introduces the series with the quaint picture of Christians likened to "beloved children" imitating (literally "mimicking") God (5:1-17). It suggests a small child bravely matching his small strides with the large ones of his father.

This walk of holiness is to be one of love, not lust (vv. 2-7); of light, not darkness (vv. 8-14); of wisdom, not folly (vv. 15-17).

Thus closes this delightful section of the Epistle regarding the walk that is "worthy of the calling with which you have been called."

It is Theodore H. Kitching who gives us these meaningful thoughts in a hymn:

How wonderful it is to walk with God
Along the road that holy men have trod!
How wonderful it is to hear Him say:
"Fear not, have faith; 'tis I who leads the way!"

How wonderful it is to talk with God
When cares sweep o'er my spirit like a flood!
How wonderful it is to hear His voice,
For when He speaks, the desert lands rejoice!

*How wonderful 'twill be to live with God
When I have crossed death's deep and swelling flood!
How wonderful to see Him face-to-face
When I have fought the fight and won the race!*

14

*What Paul said
to "the saints . . . at Ephesus" about being*

Spirit-filled Christians

EPH. 5:18—6:20

Again, in the light of God's eternal purpose that His children be "holy" in their character and "blameless" in their conduct (1:4), Paul calls them to be Spirit-filled.

> And do not get drunk with wine, for that is dissipation, but be filled with the Spirit, speaking to one another in psalms and hymns and spiritual songs, singing and making melody with your heart to the Lord; always giving thanks for all things in the name of our Lord Jesus Christ to God, even the Father; and be subject to one another in the fear of Christ *(5:18-21).*

Now there is here an interesting parallel, especially in the light of the charge of drunkenness toward the disciples on the Day of Pentecost. It is evident that a person filled with the Spirit may be likened to one who is drunk in that each is possessed by an ecstatic exhilaration.

The contrast, however, is immediately drawn. In drunkenness is "dissipation." The Greek noun *asotia* used here is variously also translated "riot," "excess," "debauchery," and "profligacy." As an adverb, Jesus uses it describing the prodigal son who "squandered his estate *with loose living.*" The word is derived from *a,* "negative" or "without"; and *sodzo,* "to save." It suggests *unsafe* or, theologically speaking, *unsaved.* Certainly it is all these in this context. (See 1 Cor. 6:10; Gal. 5:19-21 for condemnation of drunkenness.) But note the contrasts in results for one who is, literally, being *continually* filled and refilled with the Spirit. For the tense of the verb "filled" in the Greek is the continuing present.

1. The Christian who experiences a Spirit-filled life is not caught in riot, dissipation, debauchery, excess, profligacy, or loose living. Rather, his is the richness of Christian fellowship of spiritual songs, hymns, and music; of continual Christian thanksgiving to God for His goodness; and of thoughtful subjection to one another "in the reverence of Christ" (margin). This is the picture of the serenity of the Spirit-filled man. The debauchery of drunkenness would be vivid to those of Ephesus, where wine flowed freely. The infilling by the Spirit would also be particularly meaningful to those in Ephesus itself, with the warm memory of the great baptism of the Spirit experienced by the founders of the church four or five years before (Acts 19:1-7).

2. Now this matter of *subjection* (5:21) does not mean so much a slavish obedience, an overbearing superintendency. Rather it carries the thought of accountability, responsibility under the fear of and the reverence for, Christ. For in the final instance we *are* answerable to Him.

Thus Paul aligns the relationship of Spirit-filled persons one to another—of wives and husbands, of children and parents, of servants and masters (5:22—6:9)—as being in subjection one to another in reverence to Christ.

Wives should "be subject to your own husbands, as [you are] to the Lord," and shall also "respect" them (v. 33). The husband shall be the head of and bear a responsibility for the wife, even as Christ does for His Church. In a very solemn statement there is the edict, "Husbands, love your wives, just as Christ also loved the church and gave Himself up for her"—a sacrificial love.

Now it is significant that the command was not for the husband to love his wife with *eros*. This word does not occur in the New Testament. "In classical Greece, sensuous songs were sung in honor of the sensual, demonic deity, Eros," says George Turner. "This god was uncontrollable and yet all-controlling; the ultimate in religious ecstacy was to lose one's self-control in maddening devotion to this deity with fertility rites which often included sacred prostitution."[1] From it of course we get our word *erotic*. Yet sexual love is not unholy within the marriage bonds.

Nor did Paul command the husband to love his wife with *philia*. In normal usage this is an expression of warm friendship between two people. It is not foreign to Jesus, who thus loved Lazarus and John (John 11:3 and 20:2); nor even to God the Father, who thus loves His Son (John 5:20). No, any husband and wife should always naturally share both of these kinds of love.

Paul is here urging the husband to love the wife with *agape*, just as Christ loved the Church. This noun, says Turner, "was a colorless word in secular Greek and very seldom used." Indeed, we are told that there are only three known occurrences. "*Agape*," says G. Abbott-Smith, "is used in the New Testament to express that spiritual bond of love between man and man, in Christ, which is characteristic of Christianity. It is thus distinct from *philia* friendship (Jas. 4:4) and *eros* sexual affection, which is not used in the New Testament."[2]

Thus it is a very sacred and utterly unique relationship Paul is establishing for Christian marriage, indeed, comparable to Christ and His Church.

Undoubtedly this was based on our Lord's statement to His disciples on the eve of His departure: "A new commandment I give to you, that you love one another, even as I have loved you, that you also love one another.

By this all men will know that you are My disciples, if you have love for one another" (John 13:34-35).

Undoubtedly Paul also had in mind his own incomparable treatise on Christian love written five or six years before from Ephesus to the Corinthian church, known to us as the thirteenth chapter of First Corinthians.

But now is recorded for the first time in Sacred Writ the application of agape to the holy relationship of husband and wife. Especially in contrast to the degraded morals of the godless of his day, Paul is setting a highwater mark for godly morality, and for the Christian home.

This also is Paul's basis for the husband and wife being subject to one another in the reverence of Christ.

In the father-children relationship in the Christian home, Paul admonishes,

> Children, obey your parents in the Lord, for this is right. HONOR YOUR FATHER AND MOTHER (which is the first commandment with a promise), THAT IT MAY BE WELL WITH YOU, AND THAT YOU MAY LIVE LONG ON THE EARTH. And, fathers, do not provoke your children to anger; but bring them up in the discipline and instruction of the Lord *(6:1-4).*

Again the underlying word is *submission* in the sense of accountability one for the other and in reverence to Christ.

The same applies to the servant-master situation, which, of course, needs to be measured against the backdrop of the practices of that day.

> Slaves, be obedient to those who are your masters according to the flesh, with fear and trembling, in the sincerity of your heart, as to Christ; not by way of eye-service, as men-pleasers, but as slaves of Christ, doing the will of God from the heart. With good will render service, as to the Lord, and not to men, knowing that whatever good thing each one does, this he will receive back from the Lord, whether slave or free. And, masters, do the same things to them, and give up threatening,

knowing that both their Master and yours is in heaven, and there is no partiality with Him *(6:5-9).*

Thus does Paul establish on a very sound basis the practical, orderly, and enjoyable life of the Spirit-filled Christian in contrast to the life of debauchery of the worldling who is drunk with wine.

3. Again, in the light of God's eternal purpose toward His people that they be "holy and without blame before him in love" (KJV), he enjoins them to be warriors! (6:10-17). Spiritual Christians are not recluses, hiding from reality. They are not the spiritually "genteel"—graceful and elegant but shunning opposition, or contest, or hard work. They are not God's intellectuals, spreading a philosophy of "peace, peace; when there is no peace." No, they are warriors, facing a real and terrible foe, engaged in a life-or-death struggle. It is to be remembered that there would be vivid memories in the church of Ephesus of just such a struggle in the riot recorded in Acts 19:21 f.

Paul deals with the matter here in a forthright fashion.

a. There is the preparation. (1) The preparation of *accepting strength.* "Be strong in the Lord, and in the strength of His might" (v. 10). Or more literally according to Robertson: "Allow His power continually to be poured into you." (2) There is also the preparation of *accepting equipment:* "Put on the full armor of God, that you may be able to stand firm against the schemes of the devil" (v. 11).

b. Paul acknowledges a real enemy of terrible potency: "For our struggle is not against flesh and blood, but against the rulers, against the powers, against the worldforces of this darkness, against the spiritual forces of wickedness in the heavenly places" (v. 12).

c. Against this enemy Paul would employ "the *full* armor of God," with truth, righteousness, peace, faith, salvation, "the sword of the Spirit, which is the word of God" (vv. 13-17).

d. In view of the seriousness of the struggle, Paul finally would emphasize the power of uninterrupted, intercessory prayer "in the Spirit . . . for all the saints," and for him, "an ambassador in chains" (vv. 18-20).

Yes, the Spirit-filled man is a warrior.

And does not Christ himself say to this generation through the Word, "Be filled with the Spirit"?

> *Spirit of the living God,*
>   *Fall fresh on me.*
> *Break me, melt me, mold me, fill me;*
> *Spirit of the living God,*
>   *Fall fresh on me!*

15

*What Paul said
to "the saints . . . at Ephesus" about*

A Sanctified Church

EPH. 5:25-27

> Christ also loved the church and gave Himself up for her; that He might sanctify her, having cleansed her by the washing of water with the word, that He might present to Himself the church in all her glory, having no spot or wrinkle or any such thing; but that she should be holy and blameless.

In these carefully chosen words, Paul was restating the central theme of the Epistle, namely, that "He chose us in Him before the foundation of the world, that we should be holy and blameless before Him" (1:4). He thus bound together the entire teaching of this Epistle. Obviously, however, he was doing more. *He was now relating the sanctification of God's people to the atonement.* And this has significant, if not startling, importance.

1. His *act* was redemptive. "Christ . . . gave Himself up for her." Paul is repeating what he had just said in the second verse of this fifth chapter: "Christ also loved us [margin], and gave Himself up for us, an offering and a sacrifice to God as a fragrant aroma." He previously had written similarly to the Galatians: "Who gave Himself for our sins, that He might deliver us out of this present evil age" (1:4). As a background, Paul would be acquainted with Isaiah's statement (53:12): "He poured out Himself to

death, and was numbered with the transgressors; yet He Himself bore the sins of many, and interceded for the transgressors." He would have knowledge of the cry of John the Baptist, "Behold, the Lamb of God who takes away the sin of the world!" (John 1:29). The Redeemer was no stranger to Paul.

2. The *cause* was love. "Christ also loved the church." Nor was the love of Christ strange to Paul's writings. How eloquently he had expressed it in Rom. 5:6-8!

> For while we were still helpless, at the right time Christ died for the ungodly. For one will hardly die for a righteous man; though perhaps for the good man someone would dare even to die. But God demonstrates His own love toward us, in that while we were yet sinners, Christ died for us.

He would not be unaware of the renowned John 3:16, nor of Jesus' measure of love when He declared: "Greater love has no one than this, that one lay down his life for his friends" (John 15:13).

3. The *direction* was toward the Church. This redemptive love was expressed by God, not just for the "ungodly" world, that they might be saved; but also for the godly believers, that they might be sanctified. Paul had really expressed this fact in his personal witness to the Galatians when he said, "I have been crucified with Christ ... who loved me, and delivered Himself up for me" (2:20). He is now more inclusive—"Christ also loved the church" —all the called-out ones, the saved, the children of God. He must have been mindful of Jesus' memorable statement, "And for their sakes I dedicate Myself, that they themselves also may be sanctified" (John 17:19).

The significance of this fact should overwhelm every child of God. *He gave himself not only for me when a sinner, but also for me as a believer!*

It is to this *second* objective of the atonement that Paul is here directing his thoughts to the Ephesians. The purpose of the text is the cleansing and the sanctifying of the Church and the believer. Actually, it is only through the experience of *sanctification* that we (1:4) who as believers constitute the Church (5:27) may become "holy and blameless."

4. The *pattern* of this sanctification was to be an *event,* an occurrence, in the life of the believer, a crisis experience. For the tense of the verb "might sanctify" is aorist, the tense of a specific occurrence. It is the tense consistently used elsewhere for the act of entire sanctification in such instances already examined, as John 17:17; 1 Thess. 3:13; 5:23; 2 Cor. 7:1; Rom. 6:6; 8:2; Gal. 2:20.

It is quite evident that in the mind of God the experience of entire sanctification is as precise a transaction as the experience of being born again, of being made alive together with Christ, of being forgiven our sins. That, Paul wanted to emphasize.

5. The *desired results* of this sanctifying act were twofold. "That He might present to Himself" in the ages to come, as a specific act on a great occasion (for the tense of "present" is aorist), "the church in all her glory [as His bride], having no spot or wrinkle or any such thing"—without the trace of defilement or one mark of decadence. What a day!

This, however, was dependent on the other result, namely, that, having been sanctified, the Church "should [continually] be holy and blameless," awaiting that day in the ages to come. The verb "should be" is not future, in some indefinite time to come. Rather it is in that persistent, continuing, uninterrupted present tense, which defines the *present* overcoming life of the sanctified—being consistently holy in character, blameless in day-by-day conduct. *The same present tense is also used in the master theme of the Epistle,* "That we should [continually] be holy and blameless before Him" (1:4).

It was in God's mind "before the foundation of the world," that we, the Church, after being sanctified, should day by day consistently live that life which is the normal and natural one for the child of God—the life of holiness.

> *He wills that I should holy be;*
> *That holiness I long to feel,*
> *That full divine conformity*
> *To all my Saviour's righteous will.*
> —CHARLES WESLEY

We find, in this Epistle, Paul announcing that God has had, even before the dawn of history, an unchanging, overriding purpose for His people—that they live lives holy in character and blameless in conduct. All other of God's spiritual blessings point to and support this supreme blessing.

As a "mystery" disclosed in the "latter days" it is evident that the Gentiles are included in these plans, so that the Church is interracial and international in God's sight. For this Church, Paul would invoke "the inheritance" of the "sanctified" in spiritual power, permanence, provision, perception, and plentitude.

Having established the *call* of the Christian into a holy life, Paul devotes the next section to the *walk* of the Christian in holy living—a walk that is worthy of his calling, a walk that is defined by certain restrictions and definitions, and a walk that is an imitation of God by His dear children.

Again, Paul extols the life of the Spirit-filled Christian, contrasting its ecstasy with the debauchery of him who is filled with wine. Such continuous and repeated fillings with the Spirit lead to being "subject to one another in the fear [reverence] of Christ." There is a mutual accountability which is applied to the marital relationship of man and wife, to the homelife of father and children, to the working world of slave and master.

Finally, the man who is "holy and blameless before Him" is a warrior, combating the powers of darkness and evil in a godless age, but with God-given power, panoply, and prayer.

However, to achieve this life of holiness in His child, Christ gave himself for that man, that He might, as definitely as He brought him from death to life, cleanse and sanctify His child in a specific, post-regeneration experience.

What a Saviour!

> *Spotless Lamb, oh, wilt Thou make me*
> *Always holy in Thy sight,*
> *That the dying world may see me*
> *With my life and actions right!*
> *Blessed Jesus,*
> *Cleanse and make me spotless white.*
>
> *Spotless Lamb, I bring my weakness,*
> *All my failures to the light,*
> *To the Blood for perfect cleansing;*
> *Strengthen me with holy might.*
> *Blessed Jesus,*
> *Thou canst make me spotless white.*
>
> *Spotless Lamb, Thou perfect Cleanser,*
> *Thou dost fit me for the fight,*
> *Healing, cleansing, and renewing.*
> *Now Thy will is my delight.*
> *Blessed Jesus,*
> *Thou dost make me spotless white.*

—BARBARA STODDART

16

*What Paul said
to "the saints and faithful brethren
in Christ who are at Colossae" regarding*

Resurrection Responsibilities

COL. 3:1—4:6

Colossians is contemporary with Ephesians. Both were written from the Roman prison (Acts 28:30-31) as part of the third group of Paul's letters. They bear much resemblance to each other in contents. Noteworthy is the unwavering purpose of God to provide himself with a holy people. This was expressed twice in Ephesians (1:3-4 and 5:25-27). In Colossians it is expressed in very similar words in 1:19-22:

> For it was the Father's good pleasure for all the fulness to dwell in Him, and through Him to reconcile all things to Himself, having made peace through the blood of His cross; through Him, I say, whether things on earth or things in heaven. And although you were formerly alienated and hostile in mind, engaged in evil deeds, yet He has now reconciled you in His fleshly body through death, in order to present you before Him *holy and blameless and beyond reproach.*

Note that Paul in such statements as "through the blood of His cross" and "through death" again identifies holiness as inseparably related to the atonement.

With this in mind Paul deals with the subject of entire sanctification in chapter 3 under the general theme of "Resurrection Responsibilities."

The chapter commences with an identification of those who faced these responsibilities. "If then you have been raised up with Christ . . ." Some translations (20th Century, Moffatt, *Living Bible*, NIV) correctly translate it "Since then . . ." There is a confidence in this "if." Indeed, their having been "raised up with" Christ (2:12-13) marks the people of Colossae as born-again believers (1:3-8; cf. Eph. 2:1-6). It is to these *saved people* he writes, as privileged people. And privilege brings responsibility. To those who are risen with Christ there are some clear resurrection responsibilities.

There is the responsibility for *worthy associations;* the responsibility to a *decisive separation;* and the responsibility to *godly acquisitions.*

1. The responsibility for making *worthy associations* is marked by the two verbs "seeking" and "set your mind." "If then you have been raised up with Christ, keep seeking the things above, where Christ is, seated at the right hand of God. Set your mind on the things above, not on the things that are on earth" (3:1-2).

How easily man seeks and sets his mind on the things that are on earth. Is it pleasure? Is it worldly accomplishments? Is it reputation? But these shall not be the goals of the child of God.

We were driving through the incomparable Colorado Rockies, exclaiming over the beauties disclosed at every turn in the road. Then I looked into the backseat. My 12-year-old son was deep in a comic book, quite oblivious to the stirring sights about him. Isn't that the way with a Christian who sets his mind on "things that are on earth"? These things are not necessarily sinful, nor bad, nor wicked —but they are earthy, shallow, self-centered, temporary, unrewarding.

Not so! exhorted Paul. As a child of the Kingdom you

should be seeking things "above"—the Word of God, heaven, holiness, the kingdom of God. Paul expressed it well in another of the Epistles written at this time to the people in Philippi:

> Finally, brethren, whatever is true, whatever is honorable, whatever is right, whatever is pure, whatever is lovely, whatever is of good repute, if there is any excellence and if anything worthy of praise, *let your mind dwell on these things (Phil. 4:8).*

And Jesus had pointedly said: "But [continually] seek first His kingdom, and His righteousness; and all these things shall be added to you" (Matt. 6:33).

Now the admonition to this is for a *constant* seeking, a *consistent* setting of the mind. Both verbs in Paul's counsel are in the present tense, imperative mood, indicating commands to continuous action. The translator has rightly interpreted the first ("keep seeking") but strangely missed the second ("[keep setting] your mind").

If the "resurrection with Christ" experience challenges to consistently worthwhile and day-by-day associations, it also calls for an immediate action of separation and of acquisition, both marked by the aorist tense.

2. There is the call to a *decisive separation*: "But now you also, *put* them all *aside*" (3:8).

This action by the Christian, however, is dependent on a *previous* action—a separation from certain sins in which "you also once walked, when you were living in them" (3:7)—sins of the flesh from which they parted when they became saved: "immorality, impurity, passion, evil desire, and greed, which amounts to idolatry" (3:5).

This is *initial* sanctification, a cleansing from *acquired* depravity, a separation from sins, to be expected *at conversion*. With the Christians at Thessalonica this sin had been simply listed as idolatry: "How you turned to God from idols to serve a living and true God" (1 Thess. 1:9).

With the church at Corinth the list had been longer and more explicit: fornicators, idolaters, adulterers, effeminate, homosexuals, thieves, covetous, drunkards, revilers, swindlers (1 Cor. 6:9-10). Of these, Paul said, "You were washed, but you were sanctified, but you were justified in the name of the Lord Jesus Christ, and the Spirit of our God" (v. 11). And now Paul reminds those in Colossae to "consider the members of your earthly body as dead" to these. *Such sins must be kept in the past.*

In consideration of this previous separation from the sins of the flesh, however, Paul can exhort them *now* to make a decisive separation from those sins of the spirit which, for them, emerged from the *inherited* depravity, passed on from Adam, and inherent in "the old man" or "the old self":

> But now [now that you have been raised up with Christ, now that you can consider the members of your body as dead to the sins of the flesh] you also put them all aside: anger, wrath, malice, slander, and abusive speech from your mouth. Do not lie to one another, since you laid aside the old self with its evil practices, and have put on the new self who is being renewed to a true knowledge according to the image of the One who created him *(3:8-10).*

Too many Christians have never yet discovered the impact of the "now" and the "also" of this verse in their lives. Because they no longer indulge in the flagrant sins of the flesh, they forget the equally and possibly more serious sins of the spirit. There *is* deliverance from both. Christ has intended, "through the blood of His cross," that His people might, "before Him," be "holy and blameless and beyond reproach"—now! The verb "put aside" is in the decisive aorist tense of the "now."

It is curious how the matter of lying is included here with the sins of the spirit. However, in many cultures it was not considered wrong to lie. It was probably news to the Colossian converts that lying is wrong.

But entire sanctification is not just a negative experience of separation, deliverance, cleansing. Such a vacuum would be self-destructive. Christ made this awesome truth clear in His parable of the renovated, cleansed, but empty house (Matt. 12:43-45). Entire sanctification is also a positive experience of addition.

3. There is, then, the responsibility for securing *godly acquisitions.* The verb previously used, "put aside" (v. 8), and now "put on" (v. 12) are literal descriptions of garments discarded and of garments put on. This is the picture of being clothed with a new Christian Easter outfit:

> And so, as those who have been chosen of God, holy and beloved, *put on* a heart of compassion, kindness, humility, gentleness and patience; bearing with one another, and forgiving each other, whoever has a complaint against any one; just as the Lord forgave you, so also should you. And beyond all these things *put on* love, which is the perfect bond of unity *(3:12-14).*

Note that these "garments" are not the works of our own righteousness but *the gifts of His grace.* We accept them gratefully, and so put them on. And they are capped by the chief garment—love—which is the "bond" (the garment) which holds them all together in one matching ensemble of Christian perfection. What a delightful Easter outfit!

4. There are also *bonus blessings* outlined in verses 15 and 16.

"And let the peace of Christ rule in your hearts." An alternate reading is "act as arbiter"; another, "act as umpire." In other words, let His peace make all the decisions in your heart. The text continues: ". . . to which [peace] indeed you were called in one body; and be thankful [for that]."

A second bonus blessing reads: "Let the word of Christ richly dwell within you." Robertson suggests, ". . . be at home richly within you." The text continues: ". . . with all wisdom teaching and admonishing one another with psalms and hymns and spiritual songs, singing with thankfulness in your hearts to God." What an attractive picture, reminding one of the ecstasy of the Spirit-filled Christian described in Eph. 3:18-21!

To this Paul gives another admonition toward practical holy living: "And whatever you do in word or deed, do all in the name of the Lord Jesus, giving thanks through Him to God the Father."

5. In Ephesians, Paul further admonished the Spirit-filled Christians to let this life flow naturally through their domestic affairs. So here he likewise admonishes the people of Colossae to display their "new self who is being renewed to a true knowledge according to the image of the One who created him" (v. 10), in practical, domestic holiness. To husbands and wives, to fathers and children, to slaves and masters he gives much the same direction for everyday godly living as he gave the Ephesians. This pattern of life will indeed prove that for them "Christ is all, and in all" (v. 11), through *practical, Christ-centered living.*

> *Lo, a new creation dawning!*
> *Lo, I rise to life divine!*
> *In my soul an Easter morning!*
> *I am Christ's and Christ is mine.*

17

*What Paul said
to Timothy, his "beloved son," about*

Rekindling the Charisma

2 TIM. 1:6-7

The evening of a great life is drawing to a close. The end is near, and Paul knows it. "I am already being poured out as a drink offering, and the time of my departure has come" (2 Tim. 4:6). This, Paul's last Epistle, is literally packed with invaluable spiritual counsel and sound doctrine. It is fitting then that, having examined so much of Paul's teaching on holiness, we should examine this searching counsel given by the aging Paul to young Timothy. In it is contained guidance to all of us who have received the riches of God's grace and the warmth of His Spirit—those who indeed have been wholly sanctified.

> Wherefore I put thee in remembrance that thou stir up the gift [the *charisma*] of God, which is in thee by the putting on of my hands. For God hath not given us the spirit of fear; but of power, and of love, and of a sound mind *(2 Tim. 1:6-7, KJV)*.

"The *gift* of God." A study of the Greek word *charisma*, which only of late years has found its way into the English language, is interesting and rewarding. Introduced into the New Testament by Paul, it is confined to his writings, with the lone exception of 1 Pet. 4:10. Only one of seven Greek words translated "gift," it stems from *charis*, "grace," and emphasizes the "gracious," unmerited aspect of the gift. Its predominant use, then, is for a gift of grace, a divinely conferred endowment, "especially of extraordinary operations of the Holy Spirit in the Apostolic Church, but including all spiritual graces and endowments."[1]

The word is generally in the plural. There are, for example, the "varieties of gifts" (1 Cor. 12:4) of healing, miracles, prophecy, distinguishing of spirits, tongues, interpretation of tongues, helps, administrations, etc. There are notable exceptions, however, to the plurality of gifts. Rom. 5:15-16 speaks of the "free gift," identified as "the grace of God," which counters the offense of Adam's transgression and which leads to justification. Rom. 6:23 speaks of the "gift of God" which is "eternal life," and which counters "the wages of sin," which is "death." And, here in the letter to Timothy, Paul speaks of "the gift of God" which came upon Timothy by the laying on of his hands and the hands of the presbytery.

That this happened on a given occasion which Timothy and Paul well remembered is evident from the aorist-tense verb, "hath given" (KJV). Now this *charisma* quite evidently was not the gift of a captivating personality nor of a radiant disposition. Neither was it the gift of eternal life, nor of the grace of God leading to justification. The occasion was not when Timothy became a believer. It was rather the occasion when, *as a believer,* he was prepared, empowered, and made bold for the ministry.

Let us examine the scripture recounting this in Paul's first letter to Timothy:

> Let no one look down on your youthfulness, but rather in speech, conduct, love, faith and purity, show yourself an example of those who believe. Until I come, give attention to the public reading of Scripture, to exhortation and teaching. Do not neglect the spiritual gift [the *charisma*] within you, which was bestowed upon you through prophetic utterance and with the

laying on of hands by the presbytery. Take pains with these things; be absorbed in them, so that your progress may be evident to all. Pay close attention to yourself and to your teaching; persevere in these things; for as you do this you will insure salvation both for yourself and for those who hear you *(1 Tim. 4:12-16).*

That particular *charisma* he must not "neglect," but rather must "meditate upon" (KJV). And now he must stir it up.

That gift was "the spirit," or "a spirit" (NASB), or "the Spirit" (Goodspeed), or just "spirit" in the sense that Jesus said, "God is spirit" (John 4:24). Thus, it is quite apparent that, for Timothy, this *charisma* was the Gift of the Holy Spirit. This is recognized in *The Living Bible:* "For the Holy Spirit, God's gift, does not want you to be afraid."

At any rate, the receipt of the gift was a memorable, postconversion, crisis-type experience which changed his attitude, his spirit, the very purpose of his life. Again, we note that he had previously come to show a tendency to neglect this gift—"stop neglecting" (present tense in the Greek). Presently, he was allowing the fire to die down; therefore, "stir into flame the gift" (NEB); "kindle afresh the gift" (NASB); "stir up that inner fire which God gave you" (Phillips); "rekindle the embers, fan the flame and keep [it] burning" (Amplified).

How easily the Spirit-filled Christian can neglect this gift and allow the flame to die down to faint embers! Is it because he feels too "young" to maintain such an experience? Paul had said, "Let no one look down on your youthfulness." For a Christian, this youthfulness can be in age, or in Christian experience. Some maintain that this *charismatic* experience is only for "mature" Christians. It is not so! Many a youth today is showing "an example" to the older Christian in a Spirit-filled life.

Was his neglect in failing to read or to take time for meditation, as is implied in the letter? What needs to be said to emphasize the importance of searching the Scriptures, of spending time in prayer, in taking "pains with these things"? Certainly Paul was speaking to us as well as to Timothy. This spiritual life is not automatically kept alive and shining.

So, in this second letter, Paul urges Timothy to stir his experience into a flame. And he gives to him sound reason.

"For God hath not given us the spirit of fear" (KJV). Paul uses "us," remembering when *he* had received the *charisma* of the Spirit. But this "fear" is not the usual word, *phobos,* but the unusual word, *deilia,* used as a noun only here, as a verb only in John 14:27, as an adjective in Matt. 8:26; Mark 4:40; Rev. 21:8. While *phobos* is fear, either good or bad, *deilia* is fear never in a good sense. Thus it is variously translated as "timidity," "a craven spirit," and most commonly as "cowardice." This spirit of fear is alien to the Holy Spirit. Note that on the very night after the Resurrection the disciples were huddled together and "the doors were shut . . . for fear of the Jews" (John 20:19). But when the Day of Pentecost came, these fears were scattered to the winds. Paul would remind Timothy of this.

And what causes fear?

1. Fear comes from *weakness,* uncertainty, vacillation, frustrations. From all these the disciples suffered. And the answer to these was strength, *power.* This, God had promised: "But you shall receive power when the Holy Spirit has come upon you; and you shall be My witnesses" (Acts 1:8).

But this power is not the mere flexing of spiritual

muscles, nor the unrelated incoming of a mystic Personality. This power is related to a defined experience within the heart of the person.

a. It is the power of *purity*. In his testimony before the church council in Jerusalem (Acts 15:8-9), Peter likened the purifying nature of the Holy Spirit in the heathen converts to that exhibited in their own hearts at Pentecost: "And God, who knows the heart, bore witness to them, giving them the Holy Spirit, just as He also did to us; and He made no distinction between us and them, *cleansing their hearts by faith.*"

b. It is the power of *conviction*. Jesus had said, "If I go, I will send Him [the Holy Spirit] to you. And He, when He comes [to you], will *convict* the world concerning sin, and righteousness, and judgment" (John 16:7-8). Now this conviction through the Holy Spirit works two ways. For the sinner it is the conviction of condemnation; for the Spirit-filled Christian it is the conviction of confidence. And in that confidence lies power.

c. Furthermore, it is the power of *association*. Acts 4:31 declares of the threatened disciples, "And when they had prayed, the place where they had *gathered together* was shaken, and they were all filled with the Holy Spirit, and began to speak the word of God with boldness."

Thus, in the Book of Acts, *deilia,* cowardly fear, is not the key word, but *parrēsia,* "confidence," "boldness." This word is repeated again and again (4:13, 29, 31; 9:27, 29; 13:46; 14:3; 18:26; 19:8). Paul would remind Timothy of this.

What causes fear?

2. Fear comes from *indifference;* from a spirit that is aloof, detached, self-centered, small. Certainly this characterized the pre-Pentecostal disciples. They sought their

own interests. They emphasized their own importance. And the answer to their fear was love.

After receiving the gift of the Holy Spirit, they lost themselves in a burden for the very multitudes from whom they had been hiding, and in a concern for a cripple at the gate Beautiful whom they previously had never "seen." Their baptism with the Spirit was also a baptism of love. And fear was banished. "There is no fear in love; but perfect love casts out fear, because fear involves punishment, and the one who fears is not perfected in love" (1 John 4:18). Of this, too, Paul would remind Timothy.

What causes fear?

3. Fear comes from a *confused mind*—a mind that is unclear, uncertain, suspicious, resentful. And thus had the disciples been before Pentecost. They "understood not . . . and were afraid" (Mark 9:32, KJV). But the sweeping wind of the Spirit at Pentecost came as a healing current, taking out resentment, suspicion, uncertainty. The multitude, "as they observed the confidence of Peter and John, and understood that they were uneducated and untrained men, they were marveling, and began to recognize them as having been with Jesus" (Acts 4:13). The answer to a confused mind is a *sound mind.* A sound mind chases away fear.

Now, this Greek noun translated "sound mind" in the King James is used only here in the New Testament, and is variously translated as "self-control," "self-discipline," "sound judgment," "a calm and well balanced mind." In verb form (as a participle) it is used of the demoniac healed by Jesus. "And they came to Jesus and observed the man who had been demon-possessed sitting down, clothed and in his right mind" (Mark 5:15), or *"perfectly sane"* (TLB).

At any rate, Paul was declaring that the *charisma* of

the Spirit involved sane, sound, sober thinking; a calm and well-balanced mind; sound judgment.*

Finally, let it be noted that, as the disciples had needed these qualities of love, of power, and of a sound mind to banish fear, so did young Timothy. And so do we! And they are available in God's charismatic gift to us.

This, after all, is true holiness: The Spirit of power, plus the Spirit of love, plus the Spirit of a sound mind, all three in a balanced, adequate portion! Overemphasize power and you have despotism. Isolate love and you court sentimentality. Focus on sane thinking and you foster rationalism. On the other hand, eliminate power and you have impotent wishing. Subtract love and you promote a critical self-righteousness. Drop a calm, well-balanced mind and you invite emotionalism.

No, true holiness is not a specializing in one of these, but rather a fine balance of all three, as perfectly exhibited in our Lord himself, and as adequately available to His own.

We may be sure that this admonition and guidance was immensely helpful to young Timothy. We trust that he learned, before the embers died out, that the fire of the Spirit must be regularly and prayerfully "kindled afresh," "stirred into a flame," "kept alive."

> *O Thou who camest from above,*
> *The pure celestial fire impart;*

---

*In all candor it must be noted that the charismatic gift which Timothy had previously received, which he had been neglecting, and which he now should "stir up," apparently does *not* include or in any way imply the "gift of tongues." If Timothy possessed such a gift, it was of minor importance, not worthy of being listed with these three aspects which are of major importance.

*Kindle a flame of sacred love
  On the mean altar of my heart.*

*Jesus, confirm our hearts' desire
  To work and speak and think for Thee;
Still let me guard the holy fire,
  And still stir up Thy gift in me.*
—CHARLES WESLEY

PART III:
What Others Said

18

What the writer to the Hebrews said about

The Discipline of Holiness

HEBREWS 12—13

It is generally accepted that the letter to the Hebrews was written in the late sixties and thus represents some of the more mature thinking of the apostolic period. Since its author is unknown and there is no direct reference to other New Testament writings, we are unable, however, to identify directly the influence of other doctrinal statements or proclamations. Yet the subject of discipline is certainly not unique to Hebrews.

Jesus had said, "If any one wishes to come after Me, let him deny himself, and take up his cross, and follow Me" (Matt. 16:24); and, again, "If anyone comes to Me, and does not hate his own father and mother and wife and children and brothers and sisters, yes, and even his own life, he cannot be My disciple" (Luke 14:26). Paul had written, "For if you are living according to the flesh, you must die; but if by the Spirit you are putting to death the deeds of the body, you will live" (Rom. 8:13); and again, "We who are strong ought . . . not just please ourselves" (Rom. 15:1). The Psalmist had declared, "Blessed is the man whom Thou dost chasten, O Lord, and dost teach out of Thy law" (Ps. 94:12). Then Jesus had announced, "Every branch in Me that . . . bears fruit, He prunes it, that it may bear more fruit" (John 15:2).

Thus the subject of discipline would not be unknown

to the writer. Indeed, in our scripture passage he quotes Prov. 3:11-12 as a well-known saying. But it is he who especially applies discipline to the specific subject of holiness.

There appear to be three truths taught in the context of the instruction given in these two chapters.

1. First, *God's discipline, properly received by His children, brings forth holiness.*

> You have forgotten the exhortation which is addressed to you as sons, "MY SON, DO NOT REGARD LIGHTLY THE DISCIPLINE OF THE LORD, NOR FAINT WHEN YOU ARE REPROVED BY HIM; FOR THOSE WHOM THE LORD LOVES HE DISCIPLINES, AND HE SCOURGES EVERY SON WHOM HE RECEIVES." It is for discipline that you endure; God deals with you as sons; for what son is there whom his father does not discipline? But if you are without discipline, of which all have become partakers, then you are illegitimate children and not sons. Furthermore, we had earthly fathers to discipline us, and we respected them; shall we not much rather be subject to the Father of spirits, and live? For they disciplined us for a short time as seemed best to them, but *He disciplines us* for our good, *that we may share His holiness.* All discipline for the moment seems not to be joyful, but sorrowful; yet to those who have been trained by it, afterwards it yields the peaceful fruit of righteousness *(Heb. 12:5-11).*

It will be observed that the word "discipline," whether as a noun or a verb, is frequently used here. Indeed, this appears to be the central passage on this subject in the whole of the Bible.

The Greek verb is *paideuō,* a development of *pais,* the word for "child" or "youth." It has a twofold meaning. There is that of teaching or training, as in Acts 7:22, "And Moses was *educated* in all the learning of the Egyptians"; in Acts 22:3, "I [Paul] am a Jew . . . *educated* under Gamaliel"; in Eph. 6:4, "And, fathers . . . bring them up in the *discipline* and instruction of the Lord"; and in 2 Tim.

3:16, "All Scripture is inspired by God and profitable for *teaching*." "Educated," "discipline," and "teaching" are all from this root word.

There is also the meaning of chastening, correcting, as in Luke 23:16, where Pilate said, "I will therefore *punish* Him and release Him"; in 2 Cor. 6:9, "as *punished* yet not put to death"; in 1 Cor. 11:32, "We are *disciplined* by the Lord in order that we may not be condemned along with the world"; and in Rev. 3:19, "Those whom I love, I reprove and *discipline*." "Punish" and "discipline" are from this root.

Undoubtedly there is some of both meanings here—teaching and chastening—though the harsher meaning of discipline as correction and even punishment is predominant in various translations. But, after all, chastening from the Lord should instruct, and His punishment should teach.

There are three things to note here about discipline.

a. First, *all* discipline, though unpleasant at the time, is ultimately profitable (v. 11). How sorely that truth needs to be heeded now! Elizabeth Manners, headmistress of Felixstowe College in Suffolk, England, with 320 girls between the ages of 11 and 19, has said, "My subject is a dirty word. But it has *ten* letters: D-I-S-C-I-P-L-I-N-E. This is the generation that has not been disciplined, that has never met the challenge of adult authority and is therefore being driven to one extreme after another, almost as though they were daring adults to stand up to them."[1] And, in this generation, discipline is also surely needed in the spiritual realm.

One of the saddest laments recorded in the Bible is the voice of David upon learning that his son Absalom—handsome, beloved, but undisciplined—had been slain when seeking his own father's life. "And the king was deeply moved and went up to the chamber over the gate and wept.

And thus he said as he walked, 'O my son Absalom, my son, my son Absalom! Would I had died instead of you, O Absalom, my son, my son!'" (2 Sam. 18:33). Surely this is but a picture of the burdened Heavenly Father grieving over the death of a rebellious son who, refusing discipline, has gone into a godless eternity.

b. True discipline is given in love (vv. 6-8). Of this Miss Manners observes, "The most important point about discipline [is] that it must be rooted and grounded in love, love that does not lavish gifts, nor freedom to please themselves, but which exercises a kind but firm authority to protect them from their own follies."[2] And it is thus our Father disciplines His children—in the firmness of love.

c. Finally, His discipline is superior to a father's, both in understanding and in purpose (vv. 9-10). "Earthly fathers . . . disciplined us for a short time *as seemed best to them,* but He disciplines us for our good, *that we may share His holiness.*" Thus the sternness of God's punishment, correction, and chastisement is exerted on His children for the eternal purpose of their sanctification, that they may share, or be partakers of, His holiness.

Consider the possible nature of His discipline. Is it hardship? heartaches? disappointments? Does it employ prodding? urging? demanding? Does it include restrictions? denial? withholding? Does it take the nature of rebuke? criticism? correction? Whatever its nature, as it comes from His hand, it is with understanding and purpose. We must believe that.

The growing of cultured pearls is one of the most fascinating industries in the world. It was a Japanese named Mikomoto who first conceived the idea of bringing young oysters out of the ocean and planting a grain of sand in their flesh so that the irritation thus set up would produce pearls.

Now there is an obvious parallel between the development of cultured pearls and the appearance of severe tests and trials in our lives, producing character and blessings.

But there is an additional thought. The greatest skill in making a beautiful pearl is in choosing the correct size of the particle to be placed in the tender young oyster. If too small, the resulting pearl is less than it might be; if too large, it can produce an imperfect pearl, or even destroy the oyster. Skill and experience are needed in choosing the size of the piece of sand.

With what skill does our Heavenly Father choose the size of our disciplines! Sometimes they may seem overwhelming. But "God is faithful, who will not allow you to be tempted beyond what you are able" (1 Cor. 10:13). If our lives are fully committed to Him in trust and confidence, and we are willing to allow Him to choose the "piece of sand," we can be assured that He will produce a "pearl of great price" for His honor and glory. In the passage being considered, this pearl is holiness—His holiness within us.

For consider the reward, the ultimate fruit of His discipline. It is not merely that we should admire His holiness, revel in its beauty, or just look upon it with awe and reverence. It is not merely that we should hunger for it, desire it, seek after it; nor even be given it, granted it, or put in trust with it. It is rather that we should *share* it.

The Greek verb *metalambanō* has the nature of "taking together in fellowship." It is used elsewhere of the sharing of food. For example, it was said of the Early Church that "they were taking their meals together with gladness and sincerity of heart" (Acts 2:46). Reverently, it means here that God and I shall *partake* of His holiness *together*. It is an awesome, challenging thought—*sharing His holiness!* But this is the reward of *His discipline*.

2. Another great truth in this passage seems to be that *holiness is developed and enjoyed through the practice of a self-disciplined life.*

> Pursue after peace with all men, and after the sanctification without which no one will see the Lord. See to it that no one comes short of the grace of God; that no root of bitterness springing up cause trouble, and by it many be defiled; that there be no immoral or godless person like Esau, who sold his own birthright for a single meal. For you know that even afterwards, when he desired to inherit the blessing, he was rejected, for he found no place for repentance, though he sought for it with tears *(Heb. 12:14-17).*

a. Here, first, is a positive *exhortation to a pursuit.* Note the verb "pursue after." It depicts a patient pursuit, an eager chase, and is the opposite of "flee" (1 Tim. 6:11). Furthermore, to "pursue after" indicates a continuing action (the tense is present).

The double object of the pursuit is "peace" and "sanctification"—peace with all men and an unfolding holiness before God. The two go together. They both demand effort in their achievement.

Furthermore, it is only through such progressive sanctification that men really see, or comprehend, the Lord in daily life. It gives a new dimension of understanding in a day-to-day experience of Him in His holiness and in His purity. With the same goal in view, Jesus had said, "Blessed are the pure in heart, for they shall see God" (Matt. 5:8). This "see" is the Greek word *horaō,* which often depicts discernment more than sight (cf. Mark 2:5; Acts 8:23). It's the "see" the blind man uses when he comprehends something and exclaims, "Oh, now I see!"

b. Here also under the strong admonition translated "See to it" is a threefold *warning against complacency.*

There is the complacency which fails to appropriate the full grace offered by God, the grace of His holiness in everyday living, and causes the person to "come short of the grace of God."

There is again the complacency that allows defilement to creep in, such as the "root of bitterness," that bitterness of spirit which may come from such things as failure; or such as envy and jealousy, disappointment and disillusionment. Such things confront even the most holy of men.

And there is also that complacency which entices one to settle for less than Christian perfection, indeed, even to sell for a "mess of pottage" his very "birthright"—the birthright to victorious living, of being "more than conquerors through him that loved us" (Rom. 8:37, KJV).

Only by a consistent life of self-discipline can the child of God enjoy and develop the life of holiness.

3. The final great truth in this passage is that *holiness is provided through the supreme self-discipline of our Lord.* "Jesus also, that He might sanctify the people through His own blood, suffered outside the gate" (Heb. 13:12).

The writer of Hebrews had just stated of Jesus, "Who for the joy set before Him endured the cross, despising the shame, and has sat down at the right hand of the throne of God" (12:2). He might well know that Luke said of Him that, even as He faced the Cross, "He resolutely set His face to go to Jerusalem" (9:51), and that Jesus himself had declared: "I lay down My life that I may take it again. No one has taken it away from Me, but I lay it down on My own initiative. I have authority to lay it down, and I have authority to take it up again" (John 10:17-18). He might also have known of Paul's statement that "Christ also loved the church and gave Himself up for her; that He might sanctify her" (Eph. 5:25-26).

It is well authenticated that of His own free will and

choice Christ, in a supreme act of self-discipline, gave himself to provide a redemption which included both justification of the sinner and also sanctification of the believer.

Discipline is indeed a key word in God's plan for sharing His holiness with us.

4. In conclusion, it should be interesting to observe something of the tenses used in this passage. The aorist tense of *a decisive act* is used of our Lord's sacrifice, *"suffered* outside the gate"; of the intended results within the believer, "that He might *sanctify* the people"; and of the directed purpose of His disciplines, "that we may [come to the moment when we actually] *share* His holiness."

On the other hand, the present tense of *continuing action* is used of the alert practice of a self-disciplined believer: *"Pursue after* peace . . . and . . . sanctification"; *"See to it* that no one come short . . . that no root of bitterness . . . that there be no immoral person like Esau."

Thus, in a fashion consistent with Jesus, with Paul, and with Peter, the writer of Hebrews declares that, at a moment in history, our Lord gave himself for His people, so that, in a moment of time, they might be sanctified (share His holiness); and then, through the daily disciplines of a holy life, they might pursue peace and holiness, resisting the insidious and destructive powers of evil.

Ruth Tracy has expressed these thoughts in her hymn:

> *Send out Thy light and Thy truth, Lord;*
> *Into my heart let them shine.*
> *Here while I'm waiting in faith, Lord,*
> *Hark to this pleading of mine.*
> *Search now my heart, do not spare it;*
> *Pour in Thy Spirit's pure light.*

Tell me the truth; I will bear it.
   Hide not the worst from my sight.

Send out Thy light; let it lead me,
   Bring me to Thy holy hill.
When from all sin Thou hast freed me,
   I shall delight in Thy will.
Jesus, Thy wounding is tender;
   Kind is the light that reveals,
Waiting until I surrender,
   Pouring the balm then that heals.

19

*What Peter said
to "the elect strangers" exhorting*

Be Ye Holy

1 PETER 1—3

In an intriguing and very meaningful manner, the early part of First Peter divides itself into three sections separated by two "therefores" (1:13 and 2:1).

The first section, 1:1-12, emphasizes the experience of regeneration, of being born again (v. 3); the second, 1:13—2:1, the experience of sanctification, of being made holy (v. 15); and the third, 2:2—3:12, the life of holiness, and living according to the standards of God.

This concise history of the believer's life is a profound summation by Peter, as the final formal teaching in the New Testament on holiness. It is undoubtedly measured against his own spiritual experiences before and after Pentecost, and is summarized in 1:14-16:

> As obedient children, do not be conformed to the former lusts which were yours in your ignorance, but like the Holy One who called you, be holy yourselves also in all your behavior; because it is written, "YOU SHALL BE HOLY, FOR I AM HOLY."

Thus we are considering one of the most profound and challenging, and yet one of the most practical, statements in the Word. Can man really be holy?—like the God who made him?

Note three elements contained in the passage—a

meaningful *pattern,* a concise *command,* and a practical *application.*

1. Consider first the concise *command.*

a. The command is *clear:* "Be holy yourselves." Now this is not a late, New Testament idea of the latter part of the first century. Peter carefully reminds his readers of this when he quotes God as saying through His leader centuries before: "You shall be holy, for I am holy." Thrice had this been recorded in Leviticus in chapters 11; 19; and 20. Thus the mind of God was clearly revealed through Moses to the children of Israel at Sinai in the very formative years of the new nation. It was to be a basic relationship and a firm standard. After nearly 16 centuries and a new covenant, God had not changed His mind.

Indeed, in a new way, Christianity, no less than Judaism, summons to holiness. But the holiness it demands is not ritualistic and outward, but spiritual and inward—the holiness of "the pure in heart." The world at last had seen, as it had never seen through the centuries, the true holiness of God—in Christ! It was not a new concept, but one developed and refined and revealed under the new covenant.

Furthermore, this is more than a suggestion, more than an invitation, more than good advice, more even than a goal. The sentence is imperative in mood. It is as clearly a command as "Honor your father and your mother," as "You shall not steal," or "You shall love the Lord your God with all your heart." And, as a command, it must be considered as carefully as the others.

Note, too, that it was addressed, not to the ungodly and the unregenerate, but to the regenerate, the saved, to those who had been "born again to a living hope" and were "protected by the power of God through faith" (1:3, 5). It was for those who had been cleansed from their "former lusts" (1:14). Actually, it could not possibly apply to the heathen, to unbelievers, or to those who were lost. And we who are God's children must today accept it as a command directed to us.

Now, it may not be the most popular command. The person might rather be known as successful, talented, popular, witty, honored, happy, capable. However, none of these qualities is necessarily excluded in being "holy." But holiness must come first. These are secondary qualities, and all fall under the banner of "Holiness unto the Lord." Indeed, to be "holy" is more precise even than being spiritual, good Christians, good church members, and even than being Spirit-filled.

And that is as God would have it be.

b. The command, moreover, is *practical*. Man was never exhorted: "As He which called you is omnipotent, so be ye omnipotent"; nor, "As He which called you is omnipresent, so be ye omnipresent"; nor, "As He which called you is omniscient, so be ye omniscient." Rather, "Be ye holy" (KJV). For man was originally created in the likeness of God—not in His omniscience, nor His omnipotence, nor His omnipresence, but in His holiness. Thus he was never expected to attain these former attributes. But he *was* and *is* expected to attain the attribute of holiness. Thus Peter in his Second Epistle 1:4 can say, "That . . . you might become partakers of the divine nature."

c. Finally, the command is *terse,* calling for immediate action. The more accurate marginal reading declares: *"Become* holy yourselves." In line with Jesus' prayer for His disciples (John 17:17) and with Paul's desire for the Thessalonians (1 Thess. 5:23), his admonition to the Corinthians (2 Cor. 7:1), and his reminder to the Romans (6:6; 8:2), the tense is aorist, the tense of a simple occurrence. For the child of God, this should be a crisis experience, a spiritual event, as important and as precise as his conversion.

2. The *pattern* of holiness is established in the words "as he which hath called you is holy, so be ye holy" (1 Pet. 1:15, KJV).

a. Man needs a pattern, a standard, whether he is building a chicken coop, a house, or a holy life. Without it he fails.

Paul declares in 2 Cor. 10:12: "When they measure themselves by themselves, and compare themselves with themselves, they are without understanding." With Christians it is too often a game of "I am as good as she . . . better than they . . . better than I used to be." They who so measure themselves "are without understanding." They have a false measure.

A gentleman had a prized Chinese plate with curious raised figures upon it. One day it fell from the rack on which it was displayed and was badly cracked. Desiring to replace it, he sent it to China, that a copy might be made. In due time it was returned, beautifully finished with the original delicate colors, the exquisite raised figures—and the disfiguring crack.

The *Reader's Digest* carried an account of an old mountaineer who listened faithfully to a weekly radio concert by a famous violinist. One day he dispatched a peculiar request: "I have a fiddle that needs tuning. Next week when you begin your program will you sound a good, strong A, so that I can tune it?"

When the hour came, the violinist began by saying, "Old-timer, I got your letter. Get out your fiddle. Before I start my program I am going to sound for you a good, strong A." And this he did. The old-timer again tuned his fiddle to the correct pitch. Indeed, how else could the mountaineer be sure of the right pitch? He must have a proper standard to go by.

How else can a Christian be sure of his holiness? He must have a standard to go by.

b. And *that standard is the holiness of God.* It is not the holiness of an Asbury or of a Fletcher, not Booth's holiness nor Brengle's, but God's. And this opens an immense subject—the holiness of God.

In *The Wesleyan Bible Commentary,* Charles Bell, in commenting on this passage, says: "The highest incentive for personal holiness is the holiness of God. His holiness is the basic attribute of His nature. Without it His love might be partial; His power could be dangerous; His promises broken. But His holiness governs all of His perfection and action."[1]

The Bible acclaims God's holiness clearly and consistently throughout. "Who is like Thee among the gods, O Lord? Who is like Thee, majestic in holiness, awesome in praises, working wonders?" (Exod. 15:11). "Exalt the Lord our God, and worship at His holy hill; for holy is the Lord our God" (Ps. 99:9). "And one called out to another and said, 'Holy, Holy, Holy, is the LORD of hosts, the whole earth is full of His glory'" (Isa. 6:3). "Day and night they do not cease to say, 'HOLY, HOLY, HOLY, IS THE LORD GOD, THE ALMIGHTY, who was and who is and who is to come'" (Rev. 4:8).

God's holiness is defined in a negative way as an abhorrence, a loathing of sin in its every form. Habakkuk cried out, "Thou art of purer eyes than to behold evil, and canst not look on iniquity" (1:13, KJV). God's holiness is defined in a positive way as an unwavering righteousness. In the pressure of pleading for the people and the city of Sodom, Abraham confidently declared of his God: "Shall not the Judge of all the earth do right?" (Gen. 18:25, KJV).

It is a practical holiness suited to the pressures of daily living and temptation. If the command came only from a God in a distant heaven, who lacked any real feeling for His people, we might call it unjust or unrealistic. But the command came in the practical light of "the man Christ Jesus," who was "touched with the feeling of our infirmities," who was "in all points tempted like as we are, yet without sin" (KJV), and of whom it could be said that he was "holy, harmless, undefiled," and without sin. In the light of the incarnate, crucified, resurrected Lord, it is a practical holiness.

It is a holiness, furthermore, which peaked at Calvary; for only perfect love could display perfect holiness.

c. It is a holiness which requires a decisive laying aside of sins of the spirit. The sins of the *flesh,* the "former lusts which were yours in your ignorance," were overcome at the time of their conversion (1:14). That is as it should be. But Peter now speaks of overcoming sins of the *spirit.* "Therefore, putting aside all malice and all guile and hypocrisy and envy and all slander . . ." (2:1).

Consider first the verb "putting aside." It's that grammatical form (an aorist participle) which speaks of an act which has already been accomplished. For example, the same grammatical form is translated in 1:22, "Since you have . . . purified your souls." Their souls had been purified. So here, Since you have put aside the sins of the spirit. They had put them aside. But when? The answer quite obviously is when they became "holy," when they were sanctified. In short, the putting aside of the sins of the spirit is an essential part of becoming holy. And it must precede that which follows in Peter's discussion.

Now consider these so-called sins of the spirit.

"Malice" speaks of willfulness in commission of a wrong; it may speak of revengeful feelings. Malice carries a grudge. Haman showed malice not only toward Mordecai but also toward all the people of Mordecai (the Jews), and sought to destroy them all.

"Guile" points to crafty or deceitful cunning, with an emphasis on subtlety. Jeremiah described the uncleansed heart when he said: "The heart is more deceitful than all else and is desperately sick; who can understand it?" (17:9). Jesus paid Nathanael a prime tribute when He declared of him, "Behold, an Israelite indeed, in whom is no guile!" (John 1:47). Possibly Judas displayed the deepest mark of guile in his character.

"Hypocrisy" may be defined as pretense—the act or practice of pretending to be what one is not, or to espouse principles or beliefs one does not really possess or hold. Playacting! There is no sin Jesus castigates more deeply, particularly (as in Matthew 23) with respect to the scribes and Pharisees, who were the pious churchmen of that day.

"Envy" expresses the feelings of displeasure produced by witnessing or hearing of an advantage to or the prosperity of others. Envy fed the fire that burst into flame in the first murder (Gen. 4:5). Envy moved his brethren to sell Joseph into slavery and prostrate their father with grief (Gen. 37:11). And it was "because of envy" the rulers delivered Jesus up to Pilate (Matt. 27:18). No wonder David declared, "Fret not yourself because of evildoers, be not envious toward wrongdoers"; and Paul exhorted, "Let us not become boastful, challenging one another, envying one another" (Gal. 5:26). In his first letter to the Corinthians, Paul wrote: "Love is patient, love is kind, and is not jealous" (13:4).

"Slander" includes backbiting, gossip, and groundless rumor. James is particularly urgent on this subject.

> The tongue is a small part of the body, and yet it boasts of great things. Behold, how great a forest is set aflame by such a small fire! And the tongue is a fire, the very world of iniquity; the tongue is set among our

members as that which defiles the entire body, and sets on fire the course of our life, and is set on fire by hell.... If any one thinks himself to be religious, and yet does not bridle his tongue but deceives his own heart, this man's religion is worthless *(3:5-7; 1:26).*

These sins of the spirit, without question, are the bane and the despair of all too many Christians. Yet God's promise holds true: "If we confess our sins, He is faithful and righteous to forgive us our sins and to cleanse us from all unrighteousness" (1 John 1:9). These sins *can* be laid aside, cleansed. This is part of the atonement, a part of becoming "holy." And this is necessary if we are to enjoy the fruits of holiness which Peter is about to describe.

3. Peter is now ready, in the second and third chapters, to present the practical *application* of holiness as expressed in the text, "Be holy . . . in all your behavior," "in all your conduct" (RSV), "in every department of your lives" (Phillips). As Ralph Earle has observed, "An inward holiness which does not manifest itself outwardly will stand the test neither of God nor man."[2]

But let us first look again at the two "therefores" which, as previously noted, divide this portion of the letter into three sections. They appear in 1:13 and 2:1.

The first and second sections are governed by that unique Greek tense, the aorist, which marks out two spiritual events: first, of being "born again" (1:3), and then, of becoming "holy" (1:16; 2:1). These two experiences are thus displayed as separate and distinct, one succeeding the other.

The third section (2:2—3:12) is governed by the continuing present tense, and depicts the ongoing life of an everyday, growing holiness experience.

This strikingly unique arrangement of tenses merits

close attention as a framework on which Peter hung the great doctrinal truths expressed.

Furthermore, each "therefore" says, "For this reason," referring back to what has preceded. The first, in 1:13, says in essence, "For this reason—because you are begotten again as children of God—I urge you *now* to the privilege of becoming holy."

The second "therefore," in 2:1, declares, "For this reason—on the basis of your having entered into the holiness experience—I exhort you *now* to the pursuit of the new life of holy living." Thus, *one's spiritual experience is progressive and orderly, according to God's plan, not to man's invention.*

This holy behavior is presented in three aspects: in respect to themselves, in respect to God, in respect to others.

a. In a practical application of holiness in their *relationship to themselves,* they will, "like newborn babes, long for the pure milk of the word, that by it you may grow in respect to salvation" (2:2). The word "long for" is much stronger than "wish for" or "hope for." It is the same verb form as used in 1:14, and literally says "lust after." In view of the figure of speech, Phillips translates it "crying out for." They are expected to seek nourishment with great vigor—and grow!

b. In their *relationship to their God,* they will, "as living stones," be "built up as a spiritual house for a holy priesthood, to offer up spiritual sacrifices acceptable to God through Jesus Christ" (2:5). And, as "A CHOSEN RACE, A ROYAL PRIESTHOOD, A HOLY NATION, A PEOPLE FOR GOD'S OWN POSSESSION," they will "proclaim the excellencies of Him who has called you out of darkness into His marvelous light" (2:9). They will be effectual in worship and in witness.

c. In their *relationship to others,* to the world in which they live, those made holy will exhibit several traits which are characteristic of holiness.

They will, "as aliens and strangers, . . . abstain from fleshly lusts, which wage war against the soul" (2:11). They will keep their "behavior excellent among the Gentiles, so that in the thing in which they slander you as evildoers, they may on account of your good deeds, as they observe them, glorify God in the day of visitation" (2:12). They will be good examples to the world, of godliness.

As "servants" (employees), they will be "submissive to your masters [employers] with all respect, not only to those who are good and gentle [reasonable], but also to those who are unreasonable [overbearing, RSV; crooked, Robertson]" (2:18). They will show Christ at their place of employment.

As wives, sanctified women will be "submissive to your own husbands so that even if any of them are disobedient to the word they may be won without a word by the behavior of their wives, as they observe your chaste and respectful behavior" (3:1-2). They will be Christian at home.

Likewise, as husbands, holy men will "live with your wives in an understanding way, as with a weaker vessel, since she is a woman; and grant her honor as a fellow-heir of the grace of life, so that your [joint or family] prayers may not be hindered" (3:7). They will maintain a Christian marriage.

Finally, for all those who would live the holy life,

> Let all be harmonious, sympathetic, brotherly, kind-hearted, and humble in spirit; not returning evil for evil, or insult for insult, but giving a blessing instead; for you were called for the very purpose that you might inherit a blessing. For "LET HIM WHO MEANS TO LOVE LIFE AND SEE GOOD DAYS REFRAIN HIS TONGUE FROM EVIL AND HIS LIPS FROM SPEAKING GUILE. AND LET HIM

TURN AWAY FROM EVIL AND DO GOOD; LET HIM SEEK PEACE AND PURSUE IT. FOR THE EYES OF THE LORD ARE UPON THE RIGHTEOUS, AND HIS EARS ATTEND TO THEIR PRAYER, BUT THE FACE OF THE LORD IS AGAINST THOSE WHO DO EVIL" *(3:8-12).*

They will let Christ be seen in their daily lives.

This is holy living, practical and proven; this is being "holy . . . in all your behavior."

20

*What John said
to his "little children" in the Lord, concerning*

Victorious Living

1 JOHN 1—2

It seems to be very fitting to conclude this series on the high plain established by John in this Epistle, written at the end of the apostolic age. Certainly *he* was vitally aware of the teachings of Jesus regarding holiness, of the miracle of Pentecost, and of the Holy Spirit in the life of the Church. Undoubtedly he had personal knowledge of the teaching of Paul, likewise, and probably of that of Peter and of that written in Hebrews. His could very well be recognized as a summation of the practical outworkings of holiness.

Note this meaningful statement:

> My little children, I am writing these things to you that you may not sin. And if anyone sins, we have an Advocate with the Father, Jesus Christ the righteous; and He Himself is the propitiation for our sins; and not for ours only, but also for those of the whole world *(1 John 2:1-2).*

Here is a threefold treatment of the subject of victorious living under the headings: "These things," "That you may not sin," "and if."

1. "These things" are three positives.

a. First, that a God who is Light is the *Source* of victorious living: "And this is the message which we have heard from Him and announce to you, that God is light, and in Him there is no darkness at all" (1:5).

God, indeed, is that Light which, as an all-seeing Presence, reveals, searches out, and identifies. It was David who cried out:

> Where can I go from Thy Spirit?
> Or where can I flee from Thy presence?
> If I ascend to heaven, Thou art there;
> If I make my bed in Sheol, behold, Thou art there.
> If I take the wings of the dawn,
> If I dwell in the remotest part of the sea,
> Even there Thy hand will lead me,
> And Thy right hand will lay hold of me.
> If I say, "Surely the darkness will overwhelm me,
> And the light around me will be night,"
> Even the darkness is not dark to Thee,
> And the night is as bright as the day.
> Darkness and light are alike to Thee *(Ps. 139:7-12).*

Indeed, God is that Light which, as a fire, refines, purifies. Charles Wesley wrote:

> *Refining Fire, go through my heart,*
> *Illuminate my soul;*
> *Scatter Thy life through every part,*
> *And sanctify the whole!*

God is that Light which, as the Glory of God, beautifies and makes radiant, until the Psalmist invites us to "worship the Lord in the beauty of holiness" (KJV). God is also that Light which, as the Power of God, dispels fear, dread, apprehension, and the Psalmist can say: "The LORD is my light and my salvation; whom shall I fear?" (Ps. 27:1).

God is that Light which never fails. Isaiah has declared it:

> "Your sun will set no more,
> Neither will your moon wane;
> For you will have the LORD for an everlasting light,

And the days of your mourning will be finished" *(Isa. 60:20)*.

Indeed, God is the *Source* of victorious living, for "in Him there is no darkness at all."

b. The second positive among "these things" is that walking in the light is the *pattern* of victorious living: "But if we walk in the light as He Himself is in the light, we have fellowship with one another, and the blood of Jesus His Son cleanses us from all sin" (1:7).

Walking in the light indicates progress (new light day by day) and new obedience (keeping within the revealed light as it comes from Him). Walking in the light brings a twofold reward—fellowship and cleansing; fellowship with the saints and fellowship with God, plus cleansing that is constant and cleansing that is thorough.

c. The third of "these [positive] things" is that confession is the *means* of victorious living: "If we confess our sins, He is faithful and righteous to forgive us our sins and to cleanse us from all unrighteousness" (1:9).

This implies, very properly, that there is no forgiveness, no cleansing of *unconfessed sins.* On the other hand, upon confession, *full* cleansing and forgiveness are immediately available. The tense of both "forgive" and "cleanse" is the precise aorist.

2. "That you may not sin"

John wrote of "these things" for one purpose and to one specific end—that his "little children" *should not sin.* All attention now centers on this end, for it carries the very heart of victorious living. It supports the blameless life so frequently exhorted and promised elsewhere in the Word. It gives definition to entire sanctification.

Leo G. Cox has said in *The Wesleyan Bible Commentary* on this passage:

> One should never lay any limitation upon God's

> power to accomplish in His children the promise of full cleansing from sin through the blood of Christ. Any excuse for or allowance of the continuance of sin in the life of the believer is contrary to God's will for Christians, and places a limitation upon the power of the cross of Jesus. God promises, not only the *sovereign pardon* for all sins committed, but also the *complete cleansing* of all indwelling pollution in the believer. The possession of a clean heart before God fulfills for the Christian the gracious promise of the Father in Acts 1:5-8.[1]

Practical holiness is not something that begins by *doing,* but by *being.* Holiness works from the heart out to the surface. It must start within:

"That you may not sin." This is a privilege, and an opportunity. It really isn't an edict from God. It is not so much a command as it is a right, a prerogative, a privilege. The opportunity, the choice, but also the responsibility are yours.

Whatever else it is, it is also God's standard for victorious living. Sometimes God's children play lightly with sins and sinning. God doesn't. The tense again, is aorist, which would make the phrase mean: "That you may not sin *at all,* not even once!" Dean Alford is credited with saying of this verse: "The Greek implies an absence, not only of the habit of sin, but of single acts of sin."

Christians are not to sin, period. Someone has well said: "To say that I have not sinned is to make Him a liar; to say that I must sin is to destroy the fundamentals of Christianity; to say that I cannot sin is to deceive myself; but to say that *I need not sin* is to acknowledge the divine provision of Calvary." Sin, even one sin, is not the *normal* act of the child of God.

Charles Wesley wrote:

> *All things are possible to him*
> *That can in Jesus' name believe.*

> *Lord, I no more Thy truth blaspheme;*
>   *Thy truth I lovingly receive;*
> *I can, I do believe in Thee;*
> *All things are possible to me.*
>
> *The most impossible of all*
>   *Is that I e'er from sin should cease.*
> *Yet it shall be; I know it shall.*
>   *Jesus, look to Thy faithfulness!*
> *If nothing is too hard for Thee,*
> *All things are possible to me.*
> *Though earth and hell the word gainsay,*
> *The Word of God can never fail.*

It will be well, immediately, to contrast this statement in 2:1, dealing with a single sin, with statements made in 3:6, 9 and 5:18, dealing with habitual or repeated sins, where there is the present tense of continued action. Take 3:9: "No one who is born of God practices sin, because His seed abides in him; and he cannot [practice] sin, because he is born of God." Habitual sinning is incompatible with the presence of God's seed, and is impossible for a true child of God. However, persist in sin and one forfeits His seed and renounces his sonship. One or the other must be relinquished.

3. The third statement of the text reads: "And if anyone sins . . ."

It is a comfort to us that John adds this. David declared: "For He Himself knows our frame; He is mindful that we are but dust" (Ps. 103:14), while Paul proclaims, "But we have this treasure in earthen vessels" (2 Cor. 4:7).

Note the circumstances established. It is the "if" of possibility—*ean*, as in 1:7, "If we walk . . ."; 1:8, "If we say . . ."; 1:9, "If we confess . . ."; 1:10, "If we say . . ." It is not the "if" of probability or assurance, *ei*, as in 4:11, "Beloved, if [since] God so loved us . . ."

Note, too, the circumstance of person. It is "anyone," singular—an occasional person, not "everyone." It is an inclusive pronoun. He does *not* say, *"Since* everyone sins in word and deed and thought every day." The NEB accurately translates it: "But should anyone commit a sin." Literally, John is declaring, "If it should come to pass that an individual should commit a sin . . ." John is not dealing with the sinning world, nor, indeed, with the careless or the rebellious backslider who returns to a life of sin. He deals with *the believer who finds himself in a sin.*

And how does a devout Christian find himself in a sin? There may be many ways: by yielding to temptation, as did Adam; by turning isolated "thoughts about evil" into a stream of "evil thoughts" (Mark 7:21-22); by starving his soul (1 Pet. 2:1-2); by failing to live up to revealed light (1 John 1:7); by failing to do what one knows he should do (Jas. 4:17). (See also 1 Sam. 12:23.) The most holy of men can find himself in a sin, and eventually in sins. No man is immune.

It should be pointed out that there is a difference between sin and infirmity. Deliberate sin is to be publicly rebuked (1 Tim. 5:20). Persisted in, it brings death (Ezek. 18:4). On the other hand, infirmity or weakness is to be "shared" or "borne" by those who are strong (Rom. 15:1). It will be understood and sympathized with by our great High Priest (Heb. 4:15). It may even be boasted of by him who suffers the weakness (2 Cor. 12:9-10) "that the power of Christ may dwell in me." Infirmities may bring humiliation and regret, but not guilt or condemnation.

John is dealing with sin, even though an isolated sin, which even the wholly sanctified may commit in an unguarded moment. At that point the child of God has two benefits. First, he has two *Paracletes.* Christ is his Advocate, his Intercessor before God (v. 2; Rom. 8:34; Heb. 7:25; 9:24); and the Holy Spirit is his Helper, his Counsellor within his own heart (John 14:16-17). These *Paracletes* are unique to the believer. Secondly, he has the benefit of Christ as "the propitiation" for his sin, the One who by His death on the Cross made possible man's reconciliation with God. The child of God has no unique remedy for his sin. He too must come to the Cross in repentance, together with the deepest sinner.

This should be a sobering thought. "Those who have once been enlightened and have tasted of the heavenly gift and have been made partakers of the Holy Spirit, and have tasted the good word of God and the powers of the age to come, and then have fallen away," become those who again "crucify to themselves the Son of God, and put Him to open shame" (Heb. 6:4-6). There is no ignorance here—only sheer affront to the tender mercies of Him who owns him. *As long as people continue* this willful waywardness, "it is impossible to renew them again to repentance."

Surely, then, God's child will be horrified at the thought of again imposing himself on so great a Saviour at such an awesome cost. He will avail himself immediately of the atoning sacrifice, rejoice in the enabling grace of God, and resolve never again to repeat that sin.

For to him is given the indescribable privilege that he *"may not sin"* at all. The choice is his.

Surely, with Isaac Watts, he will be constrained to cry:

> *"Were the whole realm of nature mine,*
> *That were a present far too small;*
> *Love so amazing, so divine,*
> *Demands my soul, my life, my all."*

IN SUMMARY

NEW TESTAMENT TEACHING REGARDING HOLINESS

As was suggested in the introductory chapter, it should now be apparent that there has been a fascinating unfolding of a doctrine as expounded by different persons in different years and under differing circumstances. At the same time there has been a harmony of parts which is both edifying and inspiring. While the various expositions differed in what element of the doctrine of holiness they would emphasize or enlarge upon, yet they harmonized and complemented one another in a remarkable manner. This is inexplicable except that the whole matter be Spirit-guided in the sense of true inspiration of the Word.

It was truly fulfilled as Jesus had predicted regarding the Holy Spirit: "I have many more things to say to you, but you cannot bear them now. But when He, the Spirit of truth, comes, He will guide you into all the truth; for He will not speak on his own initiative, but whatever He hears, He will speak; and He will disclose to you what is to come. . . . He shall take of Mine, and shall disclose it to you" (John 16:12-14).

As it appears, there are several salient points to the doctrine of holiness as established by our Lord which are expanded and expounded by the apostles. The following scriptural "proof texts" are all contained in the essays or "expository thoughts" already explored.

1. First, it is God's plan for all mankind, from all eternity, that man should be holy in this life, should be established in the likeness of his Creator, and should live

a blameless life before Him all the days of his life: John 17; Matt. 5:48; 1 Thess. 3:12-13; 4:1-7; Eph. 1:4; 5:27; Rom. 12:2; Col. 1:19-22; 1 Pet. 1:16.

2. Again, the recipients of God's plan of holiness were already saved persons, needing—not justification and regeneration—but sanctification. These included the disciples; the people at Thessalonica, Corinth, Rome, Ephesus, Colossae; the Hebrew Christians; and the believers to whom Peter and John wrote. Certain things are to be noted. Every group of believers had this need for holiness. It is a universal need. Holiness was offered at no time to the ungodly, the unsaved; neither was it expected at the time of conversion. It is offered clearly as an experience subsequent to salvation.

3. However, at the time of his conversion man attains a degree of holiness. This takes the form of a partial sanctification, better termed an "initial" sanctification or cleansing. This sanctification is an overcoming of *acquired* depravity—sins for which he is, himself, responsible and for which he is forgiven when he is saved. They are mentioned in several cases, and principally take the form of outward sins, often as sins of the flesh. For the Thessalonians (1:9) they are simply designated as idolatry. In speaking of the initial sanctification of the Corinthians (1 Cor. 1:2) Paul is much more specific (6:9-11). This is true likewise, it will be remembered, of the Colossians (3:5-7), while Peter speaks to his people simply about "the former lusts which were yours in your ignorance" (1 Pet. 1:14). From these the believer was cleansed at the time of his justification. Every sinner needs such a cleansing.

4. But there remains, at conversion, an element of sin as a sin principle, an *inherited* depravity, "your futile way of life inherited from your forefathers" (1 Pet. 1:18), which

is variously described. Paul, in his letter to the Romans, terms it *the* sin (cc. 5—8); and, in chapter 7, as "the [sin] principle that . . . is present in me," as "a different law," as "the law of sin which is in my members." In the chapter referring to John 17 we analyzed the evidences of the sin principle at work in the disciples, discovering such sins of the spirit as jealousy, pride, ambition, vindictiveness.

Paul was quite specific in listing these sins of the spirit to the Colossians (3:8-10), and to the Corinthians (1 Cor. 1:10-12; 3:1-4), which sins he grouped together in 2 Cor. 7:1 as "all defilement of flesh and spirit." Peter likewise made a list of some of the sins he saw in God's people (1 Pet. 2:1). In writing to the Thessalonians, Paul declares that there is something "lacking in your faith" (1 Thess. 3:10), which lack is holiness (3:13).

Thus are given to us a list of only some of the sins of the spirit related to *inherited* depravity, associated with the "old man," "the body of this death," variously described, but only too common among the children of God. From these they (and we) need the deliverance of entire sanctification.

5. The next element is most striking. Without denying that a process of sanctification from the above sins, for example, may commence at the time of conversion, each one of these expositions speaks of an experience, subsequent to the new birth, but like it in several areas. This experience is a single and complete act; it is a specific result of the atonement; it is wrought by the Holy Spirit; it is not merited by personal righteousness nor accomplished by works, but is accepted by faith in the shed blood of Christ.

The distinct crisis, the singleness of act, identified first by the "suddenly" of Acts 2:2, is inherent through all the passages by the consistent use of the aorist tense, the tense of the completed act. As noted in the Appendix more fully, this (as would be expected) is the tense also of the new birth, of the forgiveness of sin, of adoption, of reconciliation.

The passages most clearly indicating a crisis sanctification include: John 17:17; Matt. 16:24-28; 1 Thess. 3:13; 5:23; 2 Cor. 7:1; Rom. 6:6, 8, 13, 22; 8:2; Eph. 5:25; Col. 3:8, 10; 1 Pet. 1:15; 2:1; Heb. 12:10; 13:12; 1 John 1:9; 2:1.

That this is a work of grace, a provision of the atonement, is established by such verses as John 17:19; Matt. 16:24-28; Rom. 5:6; Col. 1:19-22; Eph. 5:25-27; Heb. 13:12; 1 Pet. 1:18-19. That it is accepted by faith—Acts 15:9; 26:18. That it is wrought by the Holy Spirit—Acts 1:4-8; Rom. 8:1-17; Eph. 1:13-14; 1 Pet. 1:2.

This subsequent work of grace is known by various terms. It is described as being sanctified entirely (1 Thess. 5:23; John 17:17); being made holy (1 Pet. 1:16); being established in holiness (1 Thess. 3:13); being cleansed (2 Cor. 7:1; Acts 15:9); being baptized with the Holy Spirit ("the promise of the Father," Luke 24:49; Acts 1:1-8); as sharing His holiness (Heb. 12:10); being "filled with all the fulness of God" (Eph. 3:16-19); becoming "dead to sin" (Romans 6); being "crucified with Christ" (Rom. 6:6; Gal. 2:20); being set "free from the law of [the principle of] sin" (Rom. 8:2); laying aside (Eph. 4:22; Col. 3:8); putting on (Eph. 4:24; Col. 3:12). Again note that *all these are verbs of action as a single act* or completed event, as prescribed by the aorist tense.

6. All evangelical believers hold that sanctification is a Bible doctrine accomplished through the sacrificial death of Christ, dependent on the Holy Spirit for fulfillment. But some regard it as accomplished at the time of regeneration; others, merely as a process, beginning at con-

version and continuing throughout life; others as something happening only at death. But the above summary would clearly establish God's plan for a crisis work of grace, following conversion and preceding death.

7. It will be noted from the above, also, that this work of grace is both negative and positive, both a subtraction and an addition. There are sins of the spirit to be removed. There are godly traits to be acquired.

8. This subsequent work of grace, however, quite evidently is intended to introduce a *life* of holiness, generally known as: being holy (Eph. 1:4; 5:27); being blameless (1 Thess. 3:13; 5:23; Eph. 1:4; 5:27); as victorious living (Rom. 8:37); a worthy walk (Eph. 4:1); Christian perfection (Matt. 5:48); the Spirit-filled life (John 14—16; Eph. 5:18); as a continuous or progressive sanctification (John 17:19; Rom. 12:2; 2 Cor. 7:1); as considering oneself "dead to sin, but alive to God" (Rom. 6:11).

9. The above descriptions of the holy life are typically associated with the present tense, the tense in Greek of continuation, of repetition, of linear action. It is to be a lifetime of continuous growth and development. And, as noted in the Appendix, when a Greek writer changes tenses he does it for a reason.

10. This same persistent, present tense characterizes certain *distinctives of the life* of that holiness which, according to the Scriptures, consistently follows the crisis experience of entire sanctification. These include the following:

A hunger for the Word, leading to continuous growth (1 Pet. 2:2)

An enriched worship of God (Eph. 5:19-21; 1 Pet. 2:5)

An effective witness for God (Acts 1:8; 1 Pet. 2:9)

An effective warfare for God (Eph. 6:10-20)

An evidence of holiness in all manner of life (1 Peter 2—3; Romans 12—15; Col. 3:18-25; Eph. 5:22—6:9)
The practice of a self-disciplined life (Heb. 12:14-17)
A continued or repeated infilling (Eph. 5:18)
A continual cleansing (1 John 1:7)
A progressive "perfecting" (2 Cor. 7:1)
A continuous proving (Romans 12—15)
A continued transfiguration (Rom. 12:2; 2 Cor. 3:18)

This summation, it will be recognized, describes the view known as the Wesleyan position on holiness, a scriptural position which continues to prove itself practical and practicable in this twentieth century.

In this we can only echo the words of Paul to the Thessalonians, "For this is the will of God, your sanctification."

He wills that I should holy be;
　That holiness I long to feel,
That full divine conformity
　To all my Saviour's righteous will.

Come, Saviour, come and make me whole;
　Entirely, all my sins remove;
To perfect health restore my soul,
　To perfect holiness and love.
　　　　　　　　　　—Charles Wesley

APPENDIX

I. Sanctify

In certain versions there is an unfortunate rejection of the word *sanctify* as a translation of the Greek verb *hagiadzō* and a substitution of *consecrate* or *dedicate*, or *make them your own* in the translation of John 17:17 and several other important passages. This is true in NEB, TEV, Moffatt, and others. This calls for examination.

The Greek verb *hagiadzō* has two aspects. The first is *to separate from the commonplace*. This does not involve a change in character, only in purpose and use. In this instance the verb properly is translated *consecrate* or *dedicate*. This pertains, however, to a limited number of passages in scripture. It is so, for example, in Matt. 23:17, 19 regarding the Temple consecrating the gold, the altar, and the gift. It is so in John 10:36, "The one whom the Father has consecrated and sent into the world" (Phillips).

It is also true in John 17:19, "And I consecrate myself for their sakes" (Phillips). Neither the gold, the gift, nor Christ was changed in character by the act, only established as to purpose. *Consecrate* and *dedicate* as synonyms mean to set apart or devote to a sacred purpose. But they are not synonyms of *sanctify*. See Webster's *Dictionary of Synonyms* for further discussion.

The second aspect of the verb *hagiadzō* is *to separate from the unclean*, the *unholy*, thus changing the character of the person involved. It cannot properly apply to a thing. The correct translation is *sanctify*. Furthermore, *man* can dedicate or consecrate; but only *God* can sanctify. To sanctify, says the dictionary, means to make holy, to make free from sin. This is the common use of *hagiadzō*.

It should be of interest that the Revised Standard Version originally carried the word *consecrate* as the general translation of *hagiadzō*. A protest was made by a group of scholars headed by Dr. J. A. Huffman, however, and the editors acknowledged their error and made the necessary changes adopted in later editions. The RSV now carries *sanctify* or *holy* for *consecrate* in the following important passages:

John 17:17—"Sanctify them in the truth."

Acts 20:32—The "inheritance among all those who are sanctified."

Acts 26:18—"That they may receive forgiveness of sins and a place among those who are sanctified."

Rom. 15:16—"So that the offering of the Gentiles may be acceptable, sanctified by the Holy Spirit."

1 Cor. 1:2—"To those sanctified in Christ Jesus."

1 Cor. 1:30—"Christ Jesus, whom God made our wisdom, our righteousness and sanctification and redemption."

1 Cor. 6:11—"But you were washed, you were sanctified."

1 Cor. 7:34—"And the unmarried woman or girl is anxious about the affairs of the Lord, how to be holy in body and spirit."

Eph. 5:25-26—"Christ loved the church and gave himself up for her, that he might sanctify her."

1 Thess. 4:3—"For this is the will of God, your sanctification."

1 Thess. 4:4—"In holiness and honor."

1 Thess. 4:7—"For God has not called us for uncleanness, but in holiness."

2 Thess. 2:13—"God chose you from the beginning to be saved, through sanctification by the Spirit."

Heb. 10:10—"By that will we have been sanctified."

Heb. 10:14—"For by a single offering he has perfected for all time those who are sanctified."

Heb. 10:29—"The blood of the covenant by which he was sanctified."

Heb. 12:14—"Strive for peace with all men, and for the holiness without which no one will see the Lord."

Heb. 13:12—"So Jesus also suffered outside the gate in order to sanctify the people through his own blood."

II. Tense in the Greek Verbs

In the English language, tense means primarily *time* of action—past, present, future. In the Greek language, tense may also mean *type* or *kind* of action—a completed act, or continued action. We can readily see that the type of action can be very important and definitive. It is thus thrilling to discover the precise action, not only as to time, but particularly as to type which, under the superintendence of the Holy Spirit, was specified by the inspired writer.

For further discussion of this we quote Dana and Mantey:

> Where reference is made to the Greek tenses, aorist, present and perfect, there are two fundamental ways of viewing action. It may be contemplated in single perspective, as a point, which we may call *punctiliar* action; or it may be regarded as in progress, as a line, and this we may call *linear* action. The perfect tense is a

combination of these two ideas: it looks in perspective at the action, and regards the results of the action as continuing to exist; that is, in progress at a given point. Hence the perfect has both elements, linear and punctiliar. The aorist may be represented by a dot (●), the present by a line (———), and the perfect by a combination of the two (●———).[1]

The type or kind of action of a verb is known as the *aktionsart (sort of action)* of the verb.

One becomes accustomed to recognize the type of action in reading Robertson's *Word Pictures in the New Testament,* where attention is continually drawn to its significance. One will also find reference to it and to its importance in proper hermeneutics in such commentaries as *Beacon Bible Commentary; The Wesleyan Commentary; The Evangelical Commentary;* Turner and Mantey in *The Gospel of John;* and, to a certain extent, in Jamieson, Fausset, and Brown's *Commentary on the Whole Bible.*

Whether because of the fact that the English language does not readily express such type of action and therefore translations indicating it would be awkward, or for other reasons, attention to the *aktionsart* of the verbs is not widely found in translations. George B. Williams often recognizes it. The NASB, although in the introduction disavowing the significance of a difference between the aorist and the present, often recognizes it in translation. Occasional influence of this type of action is also to be found in *The Amplified Bible* and *The Living Bible.* But in none is it consistently observed.

This is indeed regrettable. A good translation into English incorporating these subtle shades of the *type* of action, as well as the time, would render a signal service to the reader of English. That is one reason why a regular reading of the New Testament directly from the original Greek can be so rewarding.

H. Orton Wiley in his *Systematic Theology* says of the aorist tense that there is no tense like it in the English language; hence translators have found it difficult to translate.[2] But it is exceedingly rewarding when properly recognized in important texts.

It is to be noted that the aorist *aktionsart*—an experience which occurs as a single, definite, completed act—is invariably associated with the act of becoming saved. Sometimes also the perfect tense is used.

John 3:7—"You must *be born* again."

Acts 16:31—*"Believe* in the Lord Jesus, and you shall be saved."

2 Cor. 5:17—"Therefore if any man is in Christ, he is a new creature; the old things *passed away;* behold, new things *have come"* (perfect tense).

1 Tim. 2:4—"Who desires all men *to be saved* and *to come* to the knowledge of the truth."

Gal. 1:4—"Who *gave* Himself for our sins, that *He might deliver* us out of this present evil age."

Gal. 2:16—*"We have believed* in Christ Jesus, that *we may be justified* by faith in Christ."

It has been noted, chapter by chapter, and then in the summary of this book, that this same aorist tense—signifying a definite, completed act—is consistently used to express the crisis experience of entire sanctification. The significance of this is readily seen.

On the other hand, attention must be given to the *present* tense as related to continuing or progressive action. Mantey declares, "The present tense in any of its moods is the converse of the aorist tense. The aorist tense means punctiliar or summary action. The present tense means linear or durative action."

We are indebted to Daniel Steele for his helpful chapter "The Tense Readings of the Greek New Testament" in his *Milestone Papers*. Kenneth S. Wuest devotes a chapter to this in his *Practical Use of the Greek New Testament* ("The Practical Use of Tense, Mood and Voice"), in which he declares: "When a Greek uses the present tense rather than the aorist, he is going out of his way to emphasize *durative* action."[3] Note the durative action in such texts as: "But if *we walk* in the light as He Himself is in the light, *we have* fellowship with one another, and the blood of Jesus His Son *cleanses* us from all sin" (1 John 1:7). "But *grow* in the grace and knowledge of our Lord and Savior Jesus Christ" (2 Pet. 3:18).

These illustrate the *progressive sanctification* provided for and expected by God of His children.

It must be observed at this juncture that there is never progressive justification, forgiveness, regeneration. They are only punctiliar, a complete act, while sanctification includes both. You cannot become "more forgiven," "more justified," "more born again," "more regenerated," "more reconciled." But you can become "more holy," even after you have "become holy."

III. Change in Tense

The *moving from one tense to another* in a passage makes for a fascinating, rewarding study of that which is scarcely, if ever, perceptible to the reader of the English translation. But of this Mantey writes:

> A Greek writer instinctively knew what tense to use in expressing an idea accurately. The more one studies the Greek the more this conviction grows upon him. . . .
>
> Perhaps nothing has been better preserved than the idiomatic force of the tenses. The wealth of the variety in the Greek tenses was by no means an unconscious possession of the New Testament writers. Slight changes

of meaning and delicate variations are flashed back and forth in many passages. We have no right whatever to assume that these writers were using such varieties of tense in reckless carelessness. A sufficient close examination, with the genius of the tenses in mind, will generally reveal a significant reason for each variation, and the point which the student should diligently seek to understand.[4]

Consider illustrations of these "slight changes of meaning and delicate variations . . . flashed back and forth" through the changing use of the tense.

Acts 16:30-31 carries the frantic request of the jailer: "'Sirs, what must I do [present] to be saved?' And they said 'Believe [aorist] in the Lord Jesus, and you shall be saved, you and your household.'"

The jailer felt there must be something he must do, and do, and keep on doing in order that someday he might possibly be saved. He saw this doctrine of works in the heathen religions. He may have assumed it to be a part of the new faith.

The apostles replied urgently: "Believe *right now* on the Lord Jesus and right now you will be saved. It isn't many things repeatedly done over a long time; it is the decisive action of faith which you exert right now which will save you."

The happy result was that "He . . . rejoiced greatly, having believed [perfect tense] in God with his whole household" (v. 34). He believed right now, and continued to believe [which is the continuing force of the present tense].

Heb. 4:16 declares: "Let us therefore *draw near* [present] with confidence to the throne of grace, that *we may receive* [aorist] mercy and *may find* [present] grace to help in time of need."

Examine this in the light of the tenses. Let us *frequently*, regularly draw near in confidence to the throne of grace. We're always welcome there. There are two benefits to be derived. The first is mercy. Mercy is sinful man's greatest need. We come as sinners, and *instantly* we receive mercy. The second benefit is grace to live a Christian life. This is available *over and over,* in our time of need.

What delicate variations, flashing back and forth!

In the light of changing tenses, Dana and Mantey's comments on 1 John 2:1 are worth noting:

> On the question of the believer's relation to sin, it is exceedingly important to observe John's use of the present and aorist tenses in his First Epistle. In I John 2:1, he uses the aorist tense twice with the verb *hamartanein, to sin,* "My little children, I write these things to you, *hina me hamartete, in order that you won't even commit an act of sin.* And *ean tis hamarte, if anyone does commit a sin,* we have an advocate with the Father." In 3:9 he uses the present tense with the same verb: "Everybody born of God *ou poiei, does not practice,* or *continue in sin;* because his seed *menei, is abiding* in him, and he is not able to *hamartanein, continue in sin,* because he *gegenetai, has been born* of God." Thus the use of tense may often, when clearly understood, illuminate passages which in the translations seem difficult.[5]

Now watch for the application of the foregoing principles of *aktionsart* (sort of action) in the messages on holiness. It will be rewarding, thrilling, informative.

IV. FURTHER STUDY ON THE AORIST TENSE IN THE GREEK

For the reader who is interested in a more detailed study of the use of the aorist tense in this thesis, we quote rather extensively herewith from the Dana and Mantey text regarding "Regular Uses of the Aorist":[6]

> While the aorist views an action as a single whole, it may contemplate it from different angles. It may regard the action in its entirety, which we call the *con-*

stative aorist; e.g. *ezēsen, he lived*. We might represent the constative aorist in a graph thus: ⟨•⟩ . The action may be regarded from the viewpoint of its initiation, which we call the *ingressive* aorist; e.g. *apethanen, he died*. The ingressive aorist might be graphically represented thus: •⟩——— . When the action is viewed in its results, we call it the *culminative* aorist; e.g. *apekteinen, he killed*. It may be indicated in the graph: ———⟨• . These modifications of the fundamental idea present the regular uses. They appear in all four moods, and also the infinitive and participle.

From among these three uses of the aorist let us give particular attention to the textual commentary on the first, which seems to apply here.

The Constative Aorist. The use of the aorist contemplates the action in its entirety. It takes an occurrence and, regardless of its extent of duration, gathers it into a single whole. We have here the basal, unmodified force of the aorist tense. i.e. *This temple was built in forty-six years*. Jn. 2:20.

Because of the fact that the constative aorist indicates nothing relative to duration, this matter may be implied or expressed from various viewpoints in the context. We may have a constative aorist referring to a momentary action (Acts. 5:5), a fact or action extended over a period of time (Eph. 2:4), or a succession of acts or events (2 Cor. 11:25).

Note that in Acts 5:5—"Ananias fell down and breathed his last"—there is depicted "a momentary action." Remember also that 1 John 2:1 reads literally, "My little children, I write these things unto you in order that you won't even commit an act of sin." Then, as has already been noted in this book, the aorist tense is the tense invariably associated with the crisis experience of becoming saved.

The above observations are quoted to support the view taken herein that the aorist tense of "sanctify" in John 17:17 is the general notion of a happening, an event, and quite in keeping with the "suddenly" of Acts 2:2. These observations also give substance to the position that the aorist tense, consistently used for the experience of sanctification, specifically defines a momentary action, an act of grace, a distinct crisis experience comparable to becoming saved.

V. CHRONOLOGY OF THE NEW TESTAMENT

(The dates given are from the
International Standard Bible Encyclopedia)[7]

Conversion of Paul	35
First Missionary Journey	45-49
Epistle of James	before 50
Apostolic Council	50
Second Missionary Journey	50-53

First Group, Paul's Epistles

1 & 2 Thessalonians from Corinth	52 or 53
Third Missionary Journey	54-58
Paul in Ephesus	54-57

Second Group, Paul's Epistles

1 Corinthians, Galatians from Ephesus	55 or 57
2 Corinthians from Macedonia	57
Romans from Corinth	57 or 58
Arrest in Jerusalem	58
First Roman Imprisonment	61-63 or 64

Third Group, Paul's Epistles
from Prison in Rome

Colossians	62
Ephesians	62
Philemon	62
Philippians	63

Release of Paul and His Journeys
in West and East   64-67

Fourth Group, Paul's Epistles
    1 Timothy, Titus from Macedonia   65-66
    2 Timothy from Roman Prison   67
Death of Paul in Rome   67 or 68

Synoptic Gospels
Acts
Jude   before 67
Hebrews

1 & 2 Peter from Rome   64-67
Death of Peter in Rome   64-67

Fourth Gospel (John)
Revelation   from Ephesus before 100
Epistles of John

Death of John   98-100

Reference Notes

Introduction

1. H. E. Dana and Julius R. Mantey, *A Manual Grammar of the Greek New Testament* (New York: The Macmillan Co., 1947), p. ix.

2. *Ibid.*, p. 179.

Chapter 3

1. *Interpreter's Bible* (Nashville: Abingdon Press, 1957), 7:847.

2. Samuel L. Brengle, *Helps to Holiness* (New York: The Salvation Army Printing and Publishing House, 1920), p. 192.

Chapter 4

1. Ralph Earle, *Evangelical Commentary on Mark* (Grand Rapids, Mich.: Zondervan Publishing House, 1957), p. 30.

Chapter 5

1. Kenneth S. Wuest, *The Practical Use of the Greek New Testament* (Chicago: Moody Press, 1946), p. 53.

Chapter 6

1. Frederick L. Coutts, *The Call to Holiness* (London: Salvationist Publishing and Supplies, Ltd., 1957), pp. 1-3.

2. *Ibid.*, pp. 2f.

3. H. Orton Wiley, *Christian Theology* (Kansas City: Beacon Hill Press of Kansas City, 1952), 2:98.

4. Ralph Earle, *Know Your New Testament* (Kansas City: Beacon Hill Press of Kansas City, 1947), p. 121.

5. W. O. Klopfenstein, *The Wesleyan Bible Commentary* (Grand Rapids, Mich.: Wm. B. Eerdmans Pub. Co., 1965), 5:543.

Chapter 7

1. Wiley, *Christian Theology* 2:98.

2. Julian C. McPheeters, *Proclaiming the New Testament* (Grand Rapids, Mich.: Baker Book House, 1964), 6:112.

3. Daniel Steele, *Milestone Papers* (New York: Eaton and Mains, 1878), p. 107.

Chapter 8

1. Alexander Maclaren, *St. Paul's Epistle to the Romans* (Grand Rapids, Mich.: Zondervan Publishing House, 1947), p. 78.

2. E. Stanley Jones, *Victorious Living* (Nashville: Abingdon Press, 1936), p. 38.

3. *The Salvation Army Handbook of Doctrine* (St. Albans, Herts.: The Campfield Press, 1969), p. 85.

4. Benjamin Field, *Handbook of Theology* (Freeport, Pa.: The Fountain Press, 1947), p. 145.

Chapter 9

1. *The Salvation Army Handbook of Doctrine,* p. 154.

2. Roy S. Nicholson, "Holiness and the Human Element," *Insights into Holiness* (Kansas City: Beacon Hill Press of Kansas City, 1962), p. 147.

3. Louis T. Talbot, *Romans* (Wheaton, Ill.: Van Kampen Press, 1936), p. 90.

Chapter 11

1. Roy L. Laurin, *Romans, Where Life Begins* (Wheaton, Ill.: Van Kampen Press, 1954), p. 417.

Chapter 14

1. George A. Turner and Julius R. Mantey, *The Gospel of John* (Grand Rapids, Mich.: William B. Eerdmans Publishing Co., 1964), p. 31.

2. G. Abbott-Smith, *A Manual Greek Lexicon of the New Testament* (Edinburgh: T. and T. Clark, 1950), p. 3.

Chapter 17

1. Abbott-Smith, *A Manual Greek Lexicon of the NT,* p. 480.

Chapter 18

1. Elizabeth Manners, *The Vulnerable Generation: The Age of the Spock-marked Child* (New York: Coward, McCann and Feoghegan, Inc., 1971), p. 73.

2. *Ibid.,* p. 77.

Chapter 19

1. Charles Bell, *The Wesleyan Bible Commentary* 6:254.

2. Ralph Earle, *Exploring the New Testament* (Kansas City: Beacon Hill Press of Kansas City, 1955), p. 401.

CHAPTER 20

1. Leo G. Cox, *The Wesleyan Bible Commentary* 6:327.

APPENDIX

1. Dana and Mantey, *Grammar of Greek NT,* p. 179.

2. Wiley, *Christian Theology* 2:447.

3. Wuest, *Greek New Testament,* p. 53.

4. Dana and Mantey, *Grammar of Greek NT,* pp. 194, 208.

5. *Ibid.,* p. 195.

6. *Ibid.,* pp. 195-96.

7. *International Standard Bible Encyclopedia* (Chicago: The Howard-Severance Co., 1930), p. 650.

Bibliography

Abbott-Smith, G. *A Manual Greek Lexicon of the New Testament*. Edinburgh: T. & T. Clark, 1950.

Brengle, Samuel L. *Heart Talks on Holiness*. New York: The Salvation Army Printing and Publishing House, 1918.

———, *Helps to Holiness*. New York: The Salvation Army Printing and Publishing House, 1920.

Coutts, Frederick L. *The Call to Holiness*. London: Salvationist Publishing and Supplies, Ltd., 1957.

Dana, H. E., and Mantey, Julius R. *A Manual Grammar of the Greek New Testament*. New York: The Macmillan Co., 1947.

Earle, Ralph. *Evangelical Commentary on Mark*. Grand Rapids, Mich.: Zondervan Publishing House, 1957.

———, *Exploring the New Testament*. Kansas City: Beacon Hill Press of Kansas City, 1955.

———, *Know Your New Testament*. Kansas City: Beacon Hill Press of Kansas City, 1947.

Field, Benjamin. *Handbook of Theology*. Freeport, Pa.: The Fountain Press, 1949.

Geiger, Kenneth, ed. *Insights into Holiness*. Kansas City: Beacon Hill Press of Kansas City, 1962.

International Standard Bible Encyclopedia. Chicago: The Howard-Severance Company, 1930.

Interpreter's Bible, The. Nashville: Abingdon Press, 1957.

Jones, E. Stanley. *Victorious Living*. Nashville: Abingdon Press, 1936.

Laurin, Roy L. *Romans, Where Life Begins*. Wheaton, Ill.: Van Kampen Press, 1954.

Maclaren, Alexander. *St. Paul's Epistle to the Romans*. Grand Rapids, Mich.: Zondervan Publishing House, 1947.

McPheeters, Julian C. *Proclaiming the New Testament*, Vol. 6. Grand Rapids, Mich.: Baker Book House, 1964.

Manners, Elizabeth. *The Vulnerable Generation: The Age of the*

    Spock-marked Child. New York: Coward, McCann and Feoghegan, Inc., 1971.

Robertson, Archibald Thomas. *Word Pictures in the New Testament.* Nashville: Broadman Press, 1931.

Salvation Army Handbook of Doctrine, The. St. Albans, Herts.: The Campfield Press, 1969.

Steele, Daniel. *Milestone Papers.* New York: Eaton and Mains, 1878.

Talbot, Louis T. *Romans.* Wheaton, Ill.: Van Kampen Press, 1936.

Turner, George A., and Mantey, Julius R. *The Gospel of John.* Grand Rapids, Mich.: William B. Eerdmans Publishing Co., 1964.

Wesleyan Bible Commentary, The. Grand Rapids, Mich.: William B. Eerdmans Publishing Co., 1965.

Wiley, H. Orton. *Christian Theology.* 3 vols. Kansas City: Beacon Hill Press of Kansas City, 1940, 1952, 1943.

Wuest, Kenneth S. *The Practical Use of the Greek New Testament.* Chicago: Moody Press, 1946.